A Witch's
Natural History

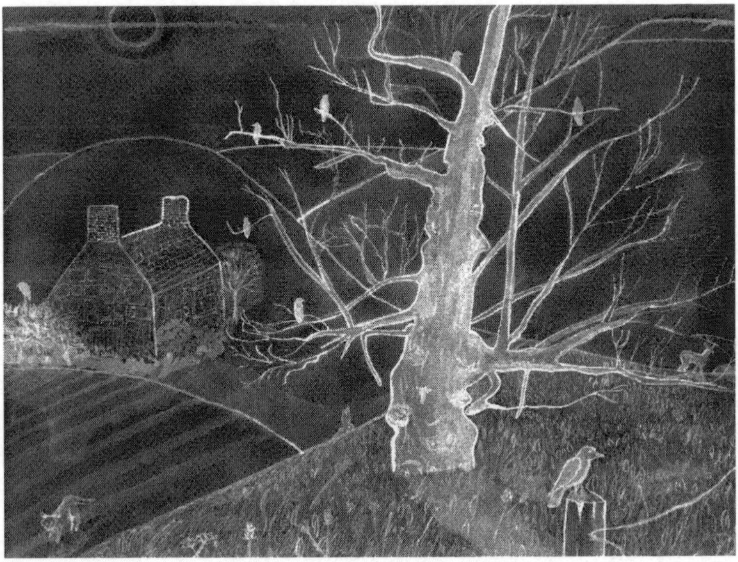

A Witch's Natural History

by
Giles Watson

With illustrations by the author

2008

TROY BOOKS

© 2008 Giles Watson

First Edition in Paperback Printed January 2013

ISBN 978-1-909602-00-7

All rights reserved.
No part of this publication may be reproduced, stored within a retrieval system or transmitted in any form or by any means, electronic, mechanical, photocopying, scanning, recording or otherwise, without the prior written permission of the author and the publisher.

Any practices or substances within this publication are presented as items of interest. The author and the publisher accept no responsibility for any results arising from their enactment or use. Readers are self responsible for their actions.

Published by Troy Books
www.troybooks.co.uk

Troy Books Publishing
BM Box 8003
London WC1N 3XX

Printed and bound in the UK

Acknowledgements

I am grateful to my father, as thoroughgoing a rationalist as ever lived, who taught me more of the awe of nature than anyone. Parts of these essays began life as poems which were originally published on his website, Michael Howard, the editor of *The Cauldron* first published these essays in his magazine, and is to be thanked for his encouragement and advice. Most importantly, these essays were written with only one audience in mind: Jeannie, who sees the world as I do.

Contents

Preface	*11*
Unfamiliar Spiders	*17*
The Witch and the Insect	*21*
Slugs, Snails and Sorcery	*29*
The Curse of the Oracle: Corvids in myth and lore	*35*
Yaffles, Gabble-Ratchets, Wudu-Snites and Assilags	*46*
'Foul and Loathsome Animals': Amphibians and the Lore of the Witch	*53*
Adder's Fork and Blind-Worm's Sting': the Magical Reptile	*65*
The Queen Rat and the Hanoverian Curse	*77*
Cryptogams: The Spore-Bearing Plants	*87*
Through the Lychgate	*95*
The Witch by the Hedge	*109*
The Witch by Moor and Wood and Shore	*119*
Beyond the Crooked Stile	*139*
Epilogue The Living Bones: A Meditation	*146*
Bibliography and Further Reading	*150*
Biographical Note	*158*
Index	*160*

Line Illustrations and Figures
By Author

Frontispiece - Uffington Poplar
Facing page - The Roebuck and the Thicket
Wryneck	15
Pisaura mirabilis	16
The Witch and the Insect	20
Downland Snail	28
The Curse of the Oracle	34
Magical Natterjack	52
Adder's Fork and Blind-Worm's Sting	65
The Queen Rat	77
Fly Agaric	86
Through the Lychgate	94
The Hedger's Craft	108
Pyramidal orchid	118
Sundew	123
Escape from Baba Yaga	132
Wayland's Smithy	139
Uprooted Beech	159

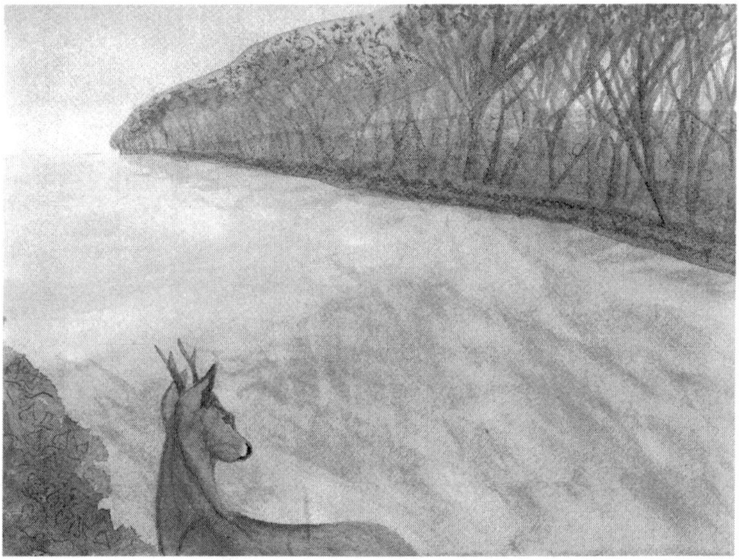

Preface

The world's dogmatic religions all have their devotional texts, whether they be explorations of mysticism such as *The Little Flowers of St. Francis* and the *Upanishads*, or hagiographies such as *The Voyage of St. Brendan*. Biological science,too, has its own rationalistic equivalents, from Darwin's own *Voyage of the Beagle* to Richard Dawkins's magnificent *The Ancestor's Tale*. Natural historians have written their works of devotion – not to a god, a philosophical system or an empirical method – but to the works of nature itself. In this country, the genre has been recognisable ever since Gilbert White wrote *The Natural History of Selborne*: it is at work in the poems of John Clare, and the essays of W.H. Hudson, Richard Jefferies and Richard Mabey. These works are all scientifically informed, but they are also brimming with spirituality, and they are all essential reading.

Witchcraft, a non-dogmatic spirituality, is steeped in nature. Divorced from the natural world, it withers into mere wordplay. Its very tools are derived from nature: wicker and withies, wooden wands, ashen stangs. One does not ride to the sabbat on a broom handle from Woolworths, but on a besom cut from living wood, with twigs hand picked from a fallen birch, bound with bark stripped from a willow bough. The very vision of the sabbat, our most precious mystery, owes itself at least in part to the judicious employment of certain plant ingredients, and is the means by which the witch communes with nature at its most potent, in the cycle of death and rebirth. Our sabbats and esbats are based around the changing seasons, and the symbols we use for these are invariably drawn from nature. Our closest spiritual companions adopt the forms of natural beings: cats, dogs, toads, rats, bats, hares, snakes, spiders. Our hidden languages arise from the lore of trees and stars. Witchcraft is just that: a Craft, a wicker basket filled with traditional ways of doing and making: neglect the weft and weave of the osier, and the basket falls to pieces.

Our Craft transcends both religion and science, but it too needs a devotional literature: devoted to its gods and spirits, certainly, but also to the natural world which is their abode as well as ours. Modern paganism regularly claims to be a "nature religion", and, rightly or wrongly, it has certainly spawned an industry which employs natural imagery lavishly and glossily. All of this is a cynical subterfuge if the individual witch knows nothing of nature. And a witch's understanding of nature cannot be theoretical and universally applicable like a scientist's: it must be rooted in the spirit of place. The witch's own environs are the locus for the practice of the Craft: they provide the tools, the inspiration, and the very spirits with whom the witch must work. A witch who does not recognise a spindle tree cannot make a spindle wand. A witch who squashes a spider without a thought squashes a part of his or her own spirituality with it. A witch who walks past a deadly nightshade plant and fails to notice it has just ignored one of our most potent symbols, and one of the most ancient simples in our apothecary. A witch who would

Preface

spurn a toad spurns the memory of Joan Prentice, Isobel Gowdie, and all the other heroes of our heritage who knew the fellowship of a familiar. A witch who forgets the earth upon which she stands, stunts her own spirit.

We would be foolish indeed to ignore the contributions science has made to our own understanding of nature. On the other hand, we must not forget that the Craft carries with it many centuries of its own natural wisdom, much of it encapsulated or encoded in folklore. A witch's natural history must be cognisant both of science and of folklore – and indeed, only a witch is likely to see why the two are not mutually contradictory; that it is not somehow spiritually schizophrenic to fight the spread of "intelligent design theory" through our schools with all the doggedness of a Dawkins, and then to pull our forelock when a single magpie passes overhead on our way home.

This little collection of essays is intended as a small contribution to modern witchcraft's devotional literature of nature, drawing on sources both scientific, folkloric and experiential. Because my own practice of the craft has been rooted in English soil, it will concentrate almost exclusively on English natural history, except where more universal aspects of witch-lore have impinged upon our understanding of nature. It will hopefully still be of use to witches whose roots are in very different soil, for they will be able to make comparisons between the world described in these pages and the world around them. The British Isles were themselves a part of the crucible from which the modern Craft arose, so that the British flora and fauna have left their impress on the Craft wherever it is practised. The ideas discussed here are therefore applicable to Craft-workers everywhere, although they must then turn to their own native soil for a lifetime's guidance. The contents of this book are in no way intended to be either definitive or systematic: this is a devotional text, not an encyclopaedia, and many of the essays included in it are more like pathworkings than field-guides.

I will say little about conservation in this book; virtually nothing about climate change. However, every sentence is written in the conviction that any magical practitioner who knows nature intimately will instinctively hear the cry of every spirit, every element, and everything that transpires or respires, to do something about both.

Preface

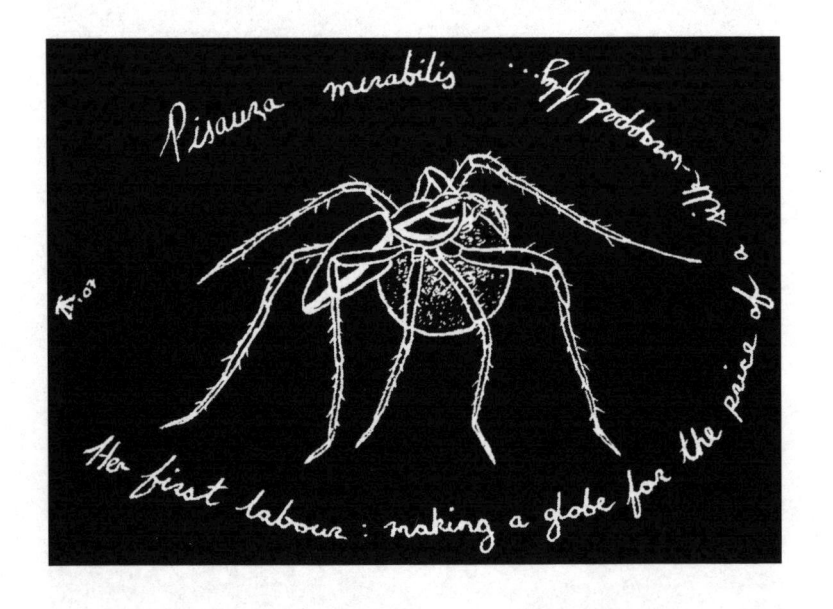

Chapter One
The Unfamiliar Spiders

One of the most enduring and archetypal characteristics of the witch is an affinity for organisms which are almost universally maligned or abused by others: toads and bats are traditional familiars, recycled *ad nauseam* in countless illustrations to children's books, and dredged up as evidence in trial records. Even the plants most used by a witch are invariably those classified as noxious weeds by everybody else. The witches of folklore transform into hares, which otherwise would arouse only the interest of gamekeepers, or into those moths which unthinking multitudes want expelled from their bedrooms before they can sleep at night. The spider, or at least her web, is part of the iconography too, but how many living witches, for all their rhetoric about the rootedness of their spirituality in natural processes, have developed any understanding of her?

Let us begin by considering the common garden spider, *Araneus diadematus*, the spinner of orb webs with the equal-sided cross on her abdomen. She is a living, esoteric jewel, whose beauty may only be appreciated by one who is not repelled by a creature with eight legs. She sits at the middle of her orb like a living compass, and when disturbed, vibrates her web at a frequency too low for our ears. She dies before her progeny are hatched, and while they are still miniscule motes, they migrate to the edges of the orb and fly away, abseiling across the heavens on their own silk. It is a journey as magical as the flight of the soul to the sabbat under the hill, a mass transvection that goes unnoticed and unvaunted year by year.

The labyrinth spider, *Agelena labyrinthica*, constructs her castle of hidden snares amongst the broken sticks and seeding inflorescences on grassy verges throughout the British Isles, a white vortex, a spun funnel leading underground. She waits at the nadir, a hopeful spinster, for her lover or her prey. The famous French naturalist Fabre knew that her nest was a castle, for he found it in the early morning, decorated with "chandeliers" of dew. How many witches have noticed? She is a dark goddess, a Lilith, a Cailleach, waiting to consume you amorously.

Search any stone wall and you will find *Euophrys frontalis*, a beautiful jumping spider with a swollen belly like a yellow gooseberry. She is courted by a diminutive male, who gestures to her in semaphore with sperm-bearing palps, and their frantic love-throes are hidden by stems of stonecrop and toadflax. Or search any hedgerow for the innumerable money spiders of the genus *Linyphia*, the arachnid balloonists par excellence, covering vast distances by means of thermals and gusts of wind. Many of them have whole series of eyes mounted on stalks, like multiple-apertured periscopes. Their chelicerae, or fangs for the uninitiated, continue to grow throughout life, so that an ageing money spider, like an old rabbit, is quite literally long in the tooth, a crone in miniature. Nearby, the male *Theridion* woos his lovers with ultrasonic stridulations, and she suspends her egg cases in a cone of gauze, a triumph in arachnid architecture, as wonderful, and sometimes as macabre, as the cottage of a Baba Yaga.

Spiders kill with superlative inventiveness. *Ero* is the pirate among spiders, sporting a bright red bandana on its bum, invading the webs of its unsuspecting victims and sucking them dry. *Scytodes thoracica*, the spitting spider, is nocturnal, and ranges widely at night in search of sleeping insects. It has additional silk glands in its foremost segment, which produce a poisonous, gummy web. It spits this in zigzags all over its slumbering victims, gluing them to the ground, then poisons them and sucks the guts out of them. It is the vampire of the spider world. The crab spider *Misumena vatia* is flower-coloured, and lurks inside roses, waiting for bees and hoverflies. Should the flower die, she moves on, and spends two days toning her hue to match that of her new residence. On goldenrod, she grows jaundiced, on holly flowers, as green as a seasick sailor, and returning to the rose, she blenches white, or blushes pink. It is her invisibility spell, and none can find the fern seed or the potion. Her venom stupefies like nightshade; her victims die in drunken agony.

Wolf spiders, *Pardosa amentata*, are solicitous mothers, carrying their eggs balled up in a woven case beneath the abdomen, and ripping it apart at the appointed time. The young clamber on the mother's back and she hunts as they ride. A larger wolf spider, *Pisaura mirabilis* hangs about in hay meadows. The male woos her with a gift of a fly wrapped in a parcel of silk. She produces a globe, an egg case, with which she trundles over meadow and furrow, grass stem and straw. She builds a web, a miniature firmament, and hangs the globe up like a moon. She watches and waits, a waning goddess. At last, she tears apart the stars, and set her angels free, their tabernacle the sky, and then she dies. And this procedure is repeated, perhaps a dozen times, perhaps more, in one meadow, by her sisters. And so on, throughout every waxing and waning year.

There is, of course, a danger in anthropomorphising like this. We run the risk of making spiders understandable, when each one is a mystery with multiple eyes. But the witch's way is the reverse of anthropomorphism. Get down on your knees, or sprawl on the ground. Dig yourself under the mould. Look on the world through the eyes of the spider. The predator, your lover and your prey are all twitches at the edge of your web. Will you venture into this world, to find out who awaits, or hide away, in the dark corner at the bottom of your bower?

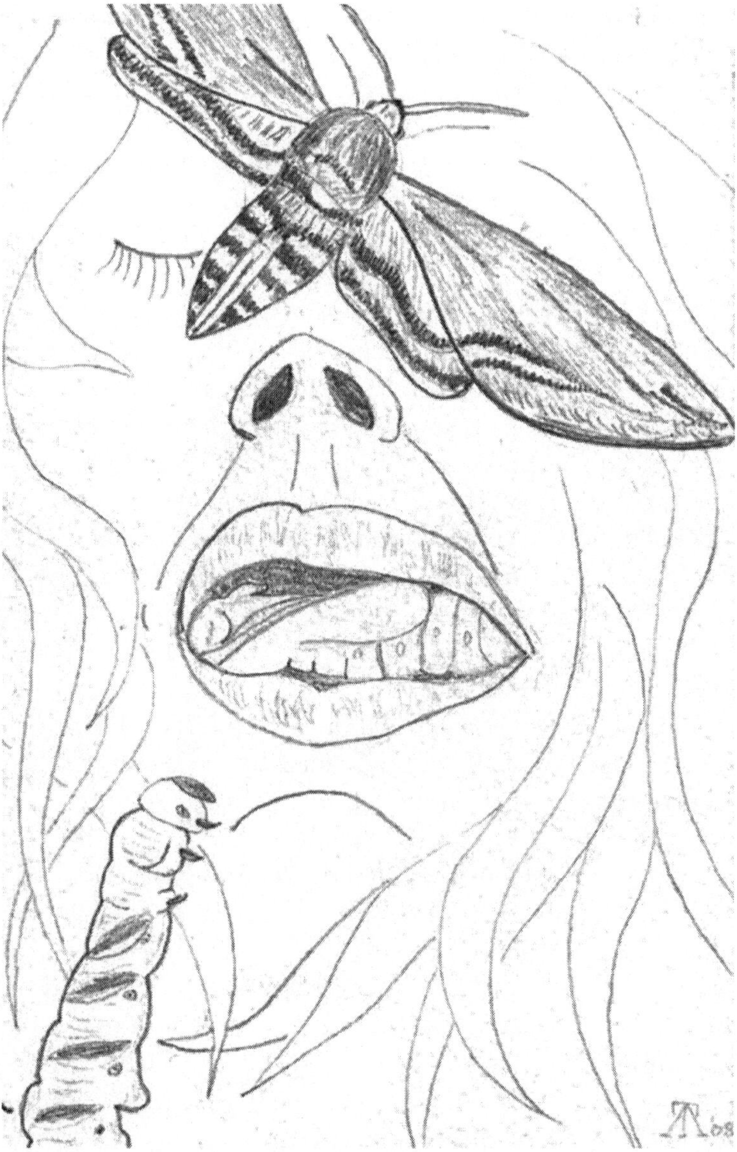

Chapter Two
The Witch and the Insect

A folk tale of the Scottish Highlands tells that Donald, a fisherman, was distracted from his dinner by the sound of a soft tapping at his window. Intrigued, he lit a cruisie and investigated the noise. A white moth fluttered against the glass, powdering it with dusty scales from its wings, so he opened the casement, and it flew into the room. It hovered briefly over the flame of the cruisie, scorched itself, and fell to the floor, whereupon it transformed into a beautiful woman, who pleaded to become his wife. Forsaking all memory of his former love, he did so, promising never to light the cruisie again, for fear that it would burn her to cinders. But his jilted lover heard his vow, and crept one night into his cottage, lighting the cruisie whilst the room was empty. When Donald's wife came into the room, her eyes bubbled into a thousand little lenses, her cloak transformed into four white wings, her tongue coiled like a watch-spring, and she fluttered into the flame. She lay seared and writhing on the floor, until Donald came into the room, and the draught from the door whisked the white moth out of the window and into the night. Donald followed after her, and was never seen again, but the white moth was found dead on the roots of a briar.

Stories of women who transform into insects are of ancient lineage. The hero of Apuleius' *The Golden Ass*, written in the second century C.E., heard the story of Cupid and Psyche, an allegory on the relationship between *eros* and *agape*. The Greek word *psyche* means both soul and butterfly, an association fostered not only by the fact that butterflies can take flight, but also by their metamorphosis from larva into imago. A similar etymological link existed in the old Lancastrian dialect, in which the word for 'soul' also meant 'moth', and it is no coincidence that one of the iconographic traditions involving transvection of witches to the sabbat depicts the soul leaving the mouth of the sleeping or inebriated witch in the form of a moth. In ancient Mexico, the god Quetzalcoatl was believed to have first entered the world in the form of a chrysalis, his emergence as a butterfly symbolising his attainment of perfection. Occasionally, the equation of *Lepidoptera* with the freedom of the soul is given a negative slant; thus in Westphalia, where butterflies are thought to be witches, children go out with hammers on St. Peter's Day, bent on the insects' destruction. Mercifully, the beauty of butterflies has arrested the spread of such cultural thuggery, and the positive image of the butterfly as a vehicle of the soul is perpetuated to this day, finding cinematic expression in the ending of Tim Burton's *Corpse Bride*.

At the end of his chapter on 'A Fairy Fauna' in his book on the South Downs, the naturalist W.H. Hudson asked himself which insect he would most like to become for a single day. Hudson considered them all: "the fantastic fly, a miracle of inconsequence"; the wasp, "that very fine insect gentleman in his mood of devilish cheerfulness"; "the grasshopper, with his small stringed instrument and long grave countenance; the dragon-fly, with those two great, gem-like orbs that reflect a nature of an unimaginable aspect." At last, he chose the common blue butterfly, because "the hue of the sky and atmosphere on this insect's wings appears to have 'entered his soul'". So far, so anthropomorphic.

The Witch & the Insect

But then, there comes a recognition which is similar to that of a shaman or a witch: "The knowledge of that strange fairy world it inhabits would be incommunicable, like a vision vouchsafed to some religionist of which he has been forbidden to speak…" Let us explore a few of these imaginative transformations.

❦

You look like a miniscule louse, climbing from an earthen hole. You ascend the swaying stems of flowers towards the sun, and stop at the stamened summit, surveying ground and grass from this wind-bent zenith. The flower shakes at the landing of an intruder, a solitary bee, and you cast off, clinging to its hairs. It takes flight, as you will never do, soaring over the heath, visiting other flowers: louseworts, bells of heather. You hold fast through all. At last, the bee comes home, to a burrow in a bank, and you are descending lower, descending only into dark Only then do you let go, and there, in the void, with a bee's egg for a raft on a sea of honey, you work destruction to ensure your survival. The egg is ripped asunder, the ocean of honey devoured. You have become a grub that is all bowel and hunger. You winter underground, bulging against the walls of the burrow, and in spring, you emerge in another guise: an articulated dream, the colour of no metal ever made, all blackness, bleared with violet oil. You devour only grass. Your head is ant-like, your antennae kinked and vibrant. You mate, and strain thousands of eggs out of the vast fecundity of your abdomen, into earthen holes beneath the swaying stems of flowers. You are the oil beetle, *Meloe violaceus*, a larval parasite of solitary bees.

Your larval days were spent inside a cowpat, which afforded all the food and shelter you required, although the diet was monotonous, and you jostled with black beetles for the softest portions. You became a pupa, entering the metamorphic slumber, awaking on the day of emergence wholly transformed. Your legs are hairy, your bristles the colour of fresh dung. The cowpat which has been your home has grown crusted and flattened, so you fly on new and gleaming wings, to seek out fresh piles among the grass and thistles. Cows blunder by, and you gad about with your companions, a merry cloud of yellow, the dung steaming and mellow beneath you. But you have grown sick of being a scatophage, and the fresh dung is no longer your food, but the bait which attracts other flies. You are a little fighter, your fuselage streamlined for speed. You grab them with your legs and eat them alive, their guts full of the dung which once sustained you. You are the yellow dung fly, *Scathophaga stercoraria*.

Your stridulence leaves the summer air shimmering and vibrant, the grasses cracking brown. Twigs snap in the shadeless heat as you woo her with the wands on your head, waving them in time with hers. As the burrs stick to ponies and to socks, and the cuckoo spit froths on the stems, you flip yourself over like a dropped pencil, and lie in the dust, bum to bum with her. Your legs grab her, caressing her slender sword, her ovipositor, and at length, you extrude a gelatinous pouch of sperm, your first and last. Pearl-coloured and viscous as a mistletoe berry, it sticks to her. Your function fulfilled, you escape the champing of her jaws to seek a slower death. In the morning, she finds your corpse, clammy in the dew, and devours it with love. You were a bush cricket, *Tettigonia viridissima*.

You look down into the water, to the algal layers, a pincer's nip from the grip of the dragon nymph, where water mites dance in miniscule, and gold-flecked tadpoles bask and gorge. There, you perform the shadow-play of mating and killing, on a surface of spilled sun. You are a film-winged skiff. Your middle legs are oars, with twin rudders at the rear. You poise on the brink, floating on the film, feeling for the tug of insects drowning. The water's skin bends, makes a meniscus you must not pierce with your predatory claws. Beneath where the water bends, your shadow blooms, like petals of a black orchid. You catch a drowning moth and suck him dry. Your lover skims bright waters to your side, your dark and flowering shadows brushing in the breeze. You are a pond skater, of the *Hydrometridae*.

A mouse lies inert on tangles of couch grass. It animates in death from backs arched beneath, as you and the rest of your verminous, altruistic horde perform the funeral rites. Where the mouse's leg hooks round a root, your mandibles leave the joint bisected. Bones are sheared through to drag the dead thing down, the charnel house lovingly prepared. The heaving soil proclaims chitin's dominion over cartilage. Your progeny lap up putrescence. You are a *Necrophorus*, a sexton beetle.

Your rival trundles through the mould, and grips you bodily, his champing jaws vice-like. He strains to flip you over, but your six clawed legs strain to push him back, and together you tumble down the leafy slope. You champ at him, and like a rutting stag, you make as if to run him through. Together, you lock in a ferocious embrace, blundering back and forth, until, in some dewy dip, you grasp him round the pronotum, and vanquish him by inverting him on the leaf litter. His legs flail for a foothold; he rights himself and retreats. The female, for whom you fought him, awaits you on the mouldering bark of a fallen branch. You mate, and fly away, thirsty for the sap of trees. You are a stag beetle, *Lucanus cervus*, an emblem of evil in early Christian art, but an inspiration to the witch. According to Norse mythology, you are the beetle of Thor, carrying glowing coals in your mandibles.

Mothlike, you remember an aquatic world of mudclouds and waterweed. You once assembled stones, twigs and snail shells to make your tubular home, and spun them together with silk from glands in your head, your body dragging behind you. You silked yourself inside, your front door like a sieve, self-imprisoned for the changing. You chew your way without, a fly with feathered legs, your last life lived at dusk. You are a caddis fly, of the order *Trichoptera*.

The tracery of dark arches is in your wings, and continued in the curve of your antennae. The mirrored cedillas, the ermine wisps, and chevrons etched in black, are like the lead of a scaled casement. The paled crux where the wings meet is the glint of moonlight through the window. All of this was once a putty-coloured worm, shearing grasses at their stems. A child grasps you, attracted by the light of your lantern, but you escape, leaving a smear of sooted scales inside her palm. You are *Apamea monoglypha*, the noctuid moth known colloquially as Dark Arches.

❊

The radical otherness of the lives of insects – their methods of reproduction, life-cycles and metamorphoses – makes them creatures of peculiar fascination to anyone who, in the words of W.H. Hudson, has a strong "sense of the supernatural in natural things". If we take beetles alone as an example, there is ample evidence of the expression of this awe throughout the ages. Paleolithic peoples, living between ten and twenty thousand years ago, fashioned pendants in the form of *Buprestid* beetles, and shamanic cultures have long revered beetles for their powers of flight, their metamorphic life histories, and their adornments of bright colours and horns. Native South American tribes from the Chaco tell stories of Aksak, a scarab who modelled man and woman out of clay. In Sumatra, the world itself is believed to be a scarab's ball of dung. Objects in the tomb of Tutankhamun were adorned with the brightly coloured elytra of beetles. Scarabs were not only revered in Ancient Egypt, but also in Minoan Crete, where votive offerings of clay beetles were made in fertility rites.

The perception that insects are somehow disgusting or inferior is a cultural construct. Children under the age of four are not alarmed by cockroaches, but after reaching that age, most will refuse a glass of water into which a plastic cockroach has been dropped, because they now associate insects with a range of cultural phobias. Before that age, children tend towards animism, which Hudson defined as "the projection of ourselves into nature". I remember, as a small child, being confronted with a female praying mantis constructing her egg case. I stared into the hazy, inscrutable black dots behind the lenses of her compound eyes, and found myself imagining my way into her world – a world in which human beings were too vast and clumsy to be bothered with, and in which a passing butterfly looks like a meal. This leap of imagination, Hudson insisted, inverting the argument of the Christian propagandist Paul, is one of the "childish things which I have no desire to put away." Nothing is more arcane and mysterious than the world of an insect, whose forebears have been on this planet at least 450 million years longer than our own. When I revel in the otherness of the insects, I know that I have always been a witch, who has refused to put away childish things.

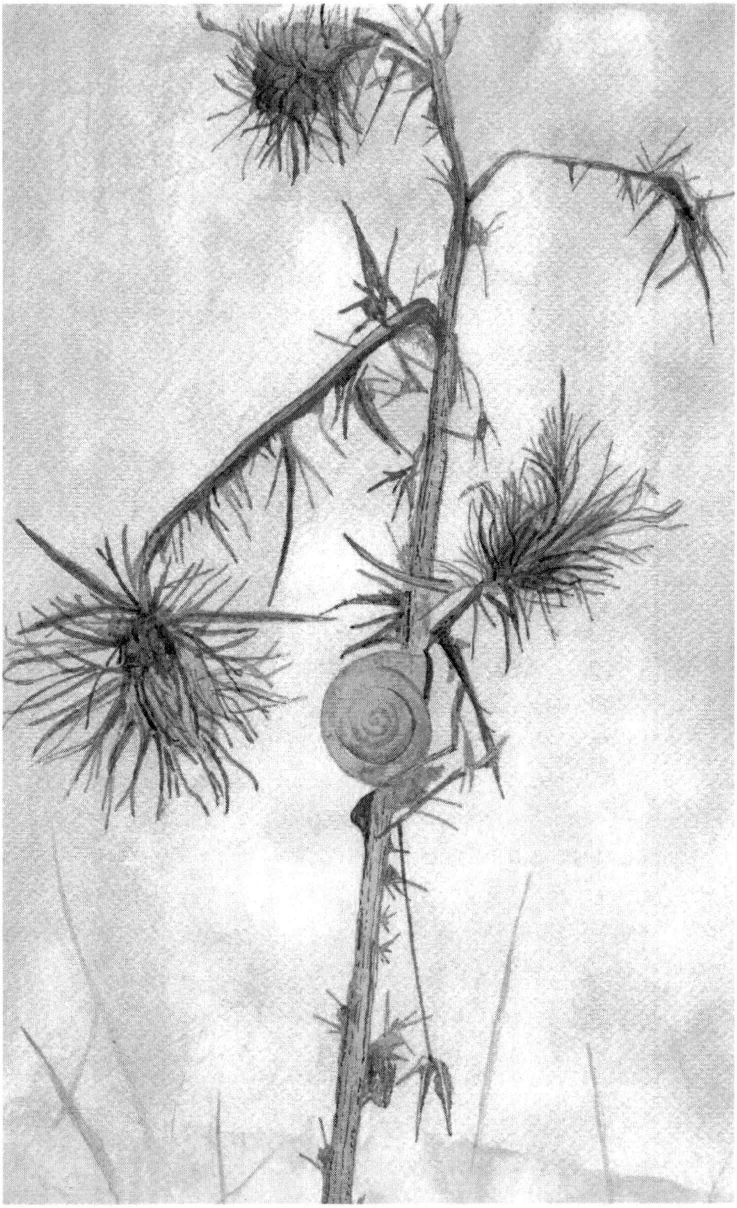

Chapter Three
Slugs, Snails and Sorcery

Perhaps the folkloric belief that garlic repels vampires has a basis in natural observation. Many human beings are attracted to the smell and taste of garlic, and of other aromatic plants such as ramsons, Jack-by-the-hedge and the three-cornered leek, but it is a reasonable assumption that predators find it repellent. Disturb a grass-snake, and it will writhe on the ground, emitting a smell of garlic, the odour of its fear. Turn a stone in a field, and the same smell may assail you without your realising its source. The tiny garlic snail, *Oxychilus allarius* has exuded it, and no doubt hopes you will find it distasteful.

It is one of the ironies of nature that gourmets now consider garlic to be the ideal accompaniment to a dish of snails. The vampire, it seems, has become immune. Perhaps it was the Romans who first gained the taste for this combination, for they were not kind to molluscs, and the trail of their conquests was marked with oyster shells. Their favourite land snail was *Helix pomatia*, which was imported to Britain by them, and still persists in the regions of Roman settlements. Roman settlers kept them in specially-built *cochlearia*, and fed them on vine leaves, and bran sodden with wine. Varro claimed to have encountered snails reared under these conditions whose shells would hold ten quarts, so perhaps Pliny was not recording his abstemiousness when he wrote that he liked to dine on barley cake, a lettuce, two eggs, sweet wine, three snails, and snow. Some of these portly snails, suspecting they were being fattened for the Bacchanalia, must have made their bids for freedom, their silver trails spanning the tessaries of the mosaic on the villa's floor, on their way towards the door. You may still find their descendents today, subsisting on meaner fare, such as nettles.

The invention of the *cochlearium* was no doubt a milestone in the development of the folklore of snails. Here, the amorousness of snails could be viewed in close proximity, and perhaps this was what led to their widespread association with sex-magic. Snails are hermaphrodites, and when they mate, they become slaves to their own ovotestes, sliming one another with love, their turgid penises wrapped in wet vaginas in mutual courtesies. Before they even come so close, they shoot little love darts of calcium carbonate, piercing each other's skin, and thereby presumably arousing passion. They are the original sadomasochists; they wrestle in giving and taking pleasure, and season it with pain. It was no doubt the close observation of this love-play which led to the practice of making love charms out of snail shells. Both gypsies and Cornish witches are fond of making such charms by stringing the shells together to form a necklace. In gypsy cultures, a girl, wanting a man she cannot have, cherishes a single shell between her breasts until it is worn and warm, then slips it into the hand of her beloved: a declaration of indelicate desire.

By the middle ages, the iconography of the dart-shooting snail had grown anthropomorphic. Snails now did battle with farmers and knights, the latter armed with spears and swords, in the margins of mediaeval manuscripts and on misericords. Such images might have been satires on chivalry, but more likely, they were sexual symbols, the softness of the snail and the sharpness of the spear being visual metaphors, reminding the viewer of the fine line that exists between pleasure and pain. There can certainly be no more apt symbol of sensuousness than a slug or a snail. Its skin can feel the presence of faint light as we can feel radiance from an open fire. It is highly sensitive to drying, and will shrink from excess of heat or cold. It has tentacles for feeling and smelling, each capable of retraction, like a finger withdrawing from a rubber glove. Its eyes, little periods on the ends of terminating stalks, inflated by excess blood, convey blurry images to the nervous system, but the sense of touch is paramount. Snails and slugs feel in full technicolour. Their skin is moist and ripe for arousal, like a lip after licking. The horns of snails have given rise to a further branch of folklore amongst gypsies and the peoples of rural England, in which they are equated with cows. They are herded by fairies, and thus become "faerie kine". Gypsies believe that the snail is the only invertebrate to win the favour of the earth fairies, and call it *Gry puvusengree*, the earthy horse. Perhaps the interrupted slime trails left by snails as their single foot undulates beneath them have led to the conclusion that they are at times ridden by the little people at a breakneck speed.

The witch who observes the minutiae of nature will be familiar with the telltale signs of the snail as victim. Thrushes make cairns of their shells, stoving them in at the apex, thrashing them mercilessly against stones. The striated, fractured shells remain for months afterwards, piled testimonies to habitual breakfasts. Fastidious bank voles are more circumspect, nibbling holes in the sides, sucking out the writhing jelly, tasting the quivering flesh with wrinkled noses, wiping their wimples afterwards. A witch who is attuned to the ways of a wood or heath may find that these piles of broken shells may assume the significance of little altars: places where creatures of habit have made immemorial meals, where countless snails have been slain. Perhaps it was the evident good health of most thrushes which led Culpepper to conclude that consumption could be cured by snail broth, to which he added purslain, violets, scabious lungwort, liquorice eclampane, annis seeds, ambrosia, white wine, the blood of a fresh-slaughtered hog, and other efficacious ingredients.

Unjustly, the folklore of slugs is comparatively impoverished. Perhaps this is merely because few people have really observed the tree slug, *Lehmannia marginata*, which is said to climb trees in order to suspend itself in slug slime, swinging beneath a branch like a chandelier made of mucus. The spotted slug, *Geomalacus maculosus*, perhaps chooses habitats which are too far flung for widespread recognition: it eats one or perhaps two species of lichen, and embodies the cliché "you are what you eat", for the fruiting bodies of the lichens themselves seem to bloom beneath its skin. We have yet to develop the requisite awe for the snail-slug (*Testacella* spp.) which, apart from sporting a tiny external shell on its rump, is a voracious carnivore fond of the living flesh of other species of slug. And we are more likely to berate the black slug *Arion ater* for devouring a recently-delivered copy of the Yellow Pages before we remembered to bring it in from the front doorstep, than we are to marvel at the sight of "half a dozen of the creatures wagging together" in irritation, as Lionel E. Adams did in 1896.

Witches, as the champions of maligned creatures, would do well to look to the slugs and snails. Perhaps it is all that mucus which so effectively repels modern antiseptic sensitivities; it ought not to disgust us. For molluscs, it is the stuff of life. A common water-snail, *Physa fontinalis*, even uses mucus as a sort of snotty tramline. Suction holds it there, perpendicular in the water: a spread thread of mucus, a wet stem of a wineglass drawn out like a wire. Watch them in a fish tank, if not in a pond: rival snails meet like Robin Hood and Little John, brandishing their horns, on the silver bridge which connects a submerged stone with the meniscus. Snails make potent sex-magic because their bodily fluids are always so clearly in evidence. Some of the most magical substances are theirs in abundance: sperm and spit and slime.

Chapter Four

The Curse of the Oracle: Corvids in Myth and Lore

There is a wood of ambivalent memory in Buckinghamshire, on the periphery of Burnham Beeches, used for duck and pheasant shooting. On weekends, the air erupts with hollow thuds of shotguns. Cartridges litter the woodland floor, some half buried amongst the beech nuts and turquoise cushions of *Leucobryum* moss. I used to go there to collect skulls, and their eye sockets would stare at visitors from the window-sill at home: a fox, several ducks, muntjacs, a squirrel, rabbits, a stoat with the brain cavity cleaved asunder, but most of all, the globed and perfect skulls of crows. Crows are intelligent, capable of tool-use and lateral thinking; pheasants are not. The gamekeeper waged war on them, incensed by the increasing inventiveness of their strategies for stealing chicks and eggs. One day, trespassing deeper into the woods, I found a dead crow slung from a barbed-wire fence, strung up like a lightning zigzag, zeroing to ground. The wings and limbs were contorted; the beak pincered the wire. Mummified in its agony, the bird had been strung up alive. Anger clouded my eyes. I cut down the corpse, dry, crisp, feather-light but still noisome, wrapped it in dark cloth and buried it in the garden, letting its blackness seep back into the earth. Later, I stood over the grave, and imagination, or an apparition, made the earth heave. An explosion of soil, and the crow burst upward in my mind's eye, over outhouses and fields, back to the wood. The gamekeeper had his own macabre sympathetic magic; I had mine.

Perhaps my love for corvids is as irrational as the gamekeeper's hatred. As a teenager, I raised baby crows, fixed the broken wings of older birds, and came at times to prefer them to human beings. I am in good company. Jackdaws, crows and magpies all have reputations as loquacious pets. A very old broken-winged currawong, a black and white Australian corvid with piercing yellow eyes, used to wander

A Witch's Natural History

around my favourite reptile park when I was a child, drawling "G'day mate" to all the tourists. Tame corvids learn quickly how to rule the roost, lording it over children, parents and pet dogs alike. They delight in stealing things and hiding them inventively, a vice which their owners are so beguiled as to consistently forgive. They imitate everything, and we echo and invoke them whenever we use their names. John Clare and Charles Dickens had pet ravens. Odin himself had two, Hugin and Munin (Thought and Memory), who flew out across the world bringing him news. The *Saga of Flokki* insists that the first mariner to discover Iceland did so by releasing his pet raven at sea and following it. A hooded crow belonging to a friend of Konrad Lorenz was trapped by a gamekeeper, escaping at the cost of one of its toes; the crow repeated the gamekeeper's words on its return. William of Malmesbury tells the story of a witch of Berkeley, in Gloucestershire, whose talking jackdaw foretold her death. Corvids are too like us, which is perhaps why they are scapegoated and hated by those who know them little enough.

There are cultures in which corvids are revered. For the Koryac, and other tribes from within the Arctic Circle, Big Raven is at once the world's creator and denizen. It is often remarked that the mischievousness of corvids is derived from boredom, like an intelligent child deprived of toys; Big Raven and his wife cure their ennui by becoming demiurges. The mountains are his excrement, and Raven himself is both celestial and earthy. His human weird is cantankerous, swallowing the sun in anger when his love-designs are thwarted, and puking it out again when he is tickled by his beloved. During a deluge, he resumes the form of a raven in order to fly to the heavens, so that he can plug up the vulva of the universe's wife, which is shedding unremitting rain. This Siberian mythos has its counterparts across the Bering

The Curse of the Oracle: Corvids in Myth & Lore

Strait, for the Raven is also regarded as a creator amongst the Inuit and the Haida tribe of the Queen Charlotte Islands.

Pre-Christian myths about corvids are characterised not by hatred, but by awe. Crows have always had the dubious honour of carrying the curse of the oracle, baring uncomfortable truths to those with too much power. In Greek mythology, the crow, originally white and personified as Cronus, was an oracular bird, and was said to house the soul of a sacred king after his sacrifice. The crow was cursed, blackened and banished by Athene after he reported to her that Herse, Pandrosos and Agraulos had plunged to their deaths from the Acropolis. Variants of this story, reinterpreted by Ovid, remain sympathetic towards the crow or raven, who is turned black for telling Apollo quite truthfully that his lover was unfaithful, and given a croaky voice for being tardy in fetching a cupful of water after being distracted by a meal of figs. A Christianised variant from the Tyrol has the child Jesus blackening the raven for soiling water he was about to drink. Perhaps this in turn was part of the genesis of allegations about Jews and witches poisoning wells.

An ancient Breton poem links corvids directly with deities. The mother of Bran, finding him dead, revived him in the form of a crow, and turned herself into a raven, so that they could spend eternity together in an old oak tree overlooking the sea. Irish and Welsh mythology emphasised the fearsome qualities of the birds, but also honoured them with divinity and superhuman powers. Badhbh, the Celtic goddess of war, united the three deities Macha, Neman and Morrigu, and manifested in a corvid form variously interpreted as a raven or a hooded crow. Her status as a deity of war is parallelled by the ancient Persian god, Verethragna, who also manifested as a raven, and who perhaps was reinterpreted as the raven attendant of Mithras. Badhbh plays a typical role in the narrative of the second battle of Moytura, in which, "after the battle was won and the corpses cleared away, the Morrigu… proceeded to proclaim that battle and the mighty victory… to the royal heights of Ireland and to its fairy hosts and its chief waters and its river-mouths" before prophesying the end of the world. A similar corvid war deity surmounts a Celtic war helmet of the second or third century BCE, found in Ciumești, Romania: a raven with hinged and flapping wings.

Cú Chulainn, too, tangled with the Morrigán in the Ulster Cycle. Woken by a shriek that could clot blood or curdle milk, the hero rushed out into the night, and was confronted by a surreal vision of a horse and chariot. The horse, blood-red in blenching moonshine, tramped on a single leg, the chariot pole pegged to his bleeding head, and rammed through his body. Beside the horse stood a woman, her eyebrows gore-tinged, her cloak dipped in dregs of battle. Beside them, a man drove a cow by hazel-fork, with tonking bell, inanely grinning. "I am Cú Chulainn, cattle-master," roared the warrior, "And you, a cow-stealer. Submit, or feel my sword." She of the reddened brow strode up to him, and riled him with riddles, till he clutched the chariot wheel and wept with rage. Her screech made mud clots in the puddles where they stood. Cú Chulainn realised that he had come out of the house bollock-naked. His wife was standing beside him, clutching his britches, sword and axe, and a chainmail suit. He turned away in embarrassment, but the chariot was gone, and on his shoulder, a croaking crow.

The supernatural awe inspired by ravens is at its most gripping in 'The Dream of Rhonabwy' from the *Mabinogion*, which tells the story of a surreal battle between the forces of Arthur and Owain's ravens. Arthur and Owain play Gwyddbwyll, with golden pieces on a silver board, the pieces reflecting their fractured faces, whilst the slaughter

The Curse of the Oracle: Corvids in Myth & Lore

continues in the valley below. Distorted raven-shadows wheel across them like windblown ash. A king's finger makes a move, its whorled print spreading and fading on yellow metal. There are cries of men and raven-cronks, flurries of black talons and wings, and the impassive faces of two kings. Skulls crash to ground, backbones fracture, spleens rupture, gashes bleed. The ravens have carried Arthur's men into the sky and dropped them from a great height, smashing their bodies against the ground. A raven yawns; a bridge of blood spans his bristled gape. The king withdraws his hand, "Your move." In all of these examples, one gets the impression that corvids were not to be shot and strung from wires, but to be propitiated and feared. Another tale from the *Mabinogion*, 'Peredur, Son of Evrawc' presents the raven's taste for carrion in a romantic light. Meeting a raven eating the corpse of a duck in the snow, Peredur sees only his beloved: the snow is the whiteness of her skin, the raven the blackness of her hair, and the drops of blood the colour of her cheeks.

Nor was the demonisation of corvids quite complete in the middle ages. A thirteenth century bestiary insists that "the raven signifies the blackness of sinners", but rather than dwelling upon this notion, proceeds to contrast the raven's supposed neglect of its nestlings with the assiduousness of the crow: "Men should teach themselves to love their children from the crow's example." However, the bestiaries were quick to deride the classical reverence for corvids: "[The Greeks] say that the crow can reveal the purpose of men's actions: it can disclose the whereabouts of an ambush, and predict the future. This is a great offence, to believe that God entrusts His counsels to crows." Christian hegemony ensured that corvids, once the oracular birds of classical and Celtic paganism, were now suitable only as auguries for the heterodox. For Shakespeare, a fearful faith in the prophetic utterances of corvids could only be suitably expressed by a villain:

> *Stones have been known to move and trees to speak;*
> *Augures and understood relations have*
> *By maggot-pies and choughs and rooks brought forth*
> *The secret'st man of blood.*
> (Macbeth, Act 3, Scene 5)

Macbeth feared that corvids would denounce him as a murderer, as in the case of the child-murderer Thomas Elks in Knockin, Shropshire, in 1590, but it was now left to witches to consort with them directly, or even to become them. Isobel Gowdie's confession (1662) included crows amongst the favourite forms taken by witches for the flight to the Sabbat. Possession of familiar crows was a sure sign of an old woman's isolation, a folk belief summed up neatly by Seldiy Bate's lyric:

> *There is a woman by the hill, if she's not dead she lives there still.*
> *The henbane all around her grows, her only friends are big black crows.*

Most damning for corvid reputations was the advent of the Black Death, which swept Europe in the mid-fourteenth century, killing between a third and a half of the population of England. Whole villages were wiped out, and survivors were often too few, or too terrified of contagion, to bury the dead. This unprecedented human tragedy can only have been a boon for carrion birds, whose taste for human flesh had previously only been indulged on battlefields and hangmen's gibbets. The sight of great flocks of black birds descending on the waste land, and picking the eyes from the skulls of one's neighbours or relatives can have done little for the estimation of corvids in the minds of survivors. It

The Curse of the Oracle: Corvids in Myth & Lore

is not surprising that by the time Pieter Breugel the Elder painted *The Triumph of Death* (1562), a crow is depicted as Death's pillion passenger, looking down on dying bodies as they are crushed beneath a cart full of skulls. The Child Ballad from the Scottish borders, 'Twa Corbies', and the more courtly English 'The Three Ravens' both dwell on corvids' appetites for the flesh of a dead knight "slain under his shield", but the corbies' agreement on how to divide the spoil may well represent a comparatively young folk memory of genuine experiences in the horrendous British winter of 1348-1349:

Ye'll sit on his white hause-bane,	*(breast-bone)*
And I'll pike out his bonny blue e'en:	*(eyes)*
Wi' ae lock o' his gowden hair	
We'll theek our nest when it grows bare.	*(thatch)*

This ballad seems to have influenced a late nineteenth century Devonshire tale in which a young woman of Brennan went to the fair, leaving her baby asleep in her garden. She saw three ravens flying from Blackingstone Rock, and asked, 'Where be you going to, ravens cruel?" "Up to Brennan!" they responded, and when she returned, her baby was gone. Its bones were later found beneath the ravens' nest on Blackingstone Rock. By the nineteenth century, it seems, the demonisation of ravens was complete. The Romans had interpreted its call as *"cras"*, Latin for tomorrow, an expression of hope. Poe's raven only says "Nevermore", a prophecy of doom.

Choughs have fared rather better in public esteem, although their popularity is perhaps in inverse proportion to their abundance. Shakespeare has hypothetical choughs picking rock samphire from the cliffs of Dover at the scene of Gloucester's attempted suicide (*King Lear*, Act 4, Scene

6), although they have not been there for centuries. The bird is proudly vaunted as the Cornish Jack, but was extinct there until only recently. It was associated with Thomas á Becket, but there are no choughs in Canterbury. It has long been vaunted as the incarnation of King Arthur, a tradition perpetuated recently not so much by the British, as by the South African poet John Trotman, whose sonnets equate the chough with Nelson Mandela. Ravens share a similar honour; the ghost of King Arthur supposedly returns annually to Badbury Rings in Dorset to relive his triumph at the battle of Badon.

Rooks too, when they are distinguished from crows at all, tend to have a more positive image; it is said, for example, that Pengersick Castle in Cornwall will fall if ever its rooks decide to leave the grounds. Their prescience is the theme of oft-reported tales of their dismantling their own nests hours before a limb drops or a tree falls – a useful skill given their fondness for nesting in elms, which tend to shed branches easily. They are still used as weather auguries in county Durham, where it is thought that if rooks feed in a village, a storm is on its way. More sinister, because it seems to akin to human behaviour, is the "parliament of rooks", a folklorically-charged phenomenon based on natural observation. Rooks may at times be seen standing in a circle in a field, as if conversing. According to some reports, two or three rooks stand in the middle of the circle, and at the end of the proceedings, either fly away looking relieved, or are set upon by the others and torn to shreds, as if they have been subjected to a trial by jury.

Jackdaws are so named because of their call, because they are smaller than other corvids, and because they are certainly the Jacks in any pack of birds; cunning, pilfering rogues. They are notorious for blocking chimneys with sticks. Accustomed as they are to nesting in hollow trees, their strategy is to drop sticks down any promising-looking hollow, until enough snag against the sides for the nest to hold. It is easy for them to provoke superstition: with daws and tchacks, the black beak clacks, toenails tapping on the chimney pot, and with his white eye in his cocked skull the little Jack blinks and bows, dropping sticks and chinking pennies into the soot. His wife lays eggs and begins to sit, but the whole lot comes clattering down the chimney, the eggs smashed, the nest collapsed, and the disgruntled jackdaw sitting in the hearth. In the north of England, such an ungainly entrance is a presage of death, the direst of omens.

Jays, with their conspicuous habit of eating and planting acorns, their near-vegetarianism besmirched only by the occasional nest-robbing escapade, and their electric-blue wing coverts, have obvious charisma. They are, however, garrulous in the extreme, and in Somerset, have earned the name Devil Scritch, along with the Gaelic *Screachag choille* and the Welsh *Ysgrech y Coed*, woodland screamers. The reference to the Devil may be more than a simple comment on the terrible racket made by a jay in the stillness of the woods. A folk tradition in the southern states of the U.S.A. insists that jays are never seen on Fridays, when they are busy taking sticks to the Devil. Perhaps jays too are still recognisably witches' birds, lending their wing coverts as charms.

The decline of gamekeeping, which has to a certain extent led to the rehabilitation of corvid reputations, has not helped the popular cause of the highly successful English magpie. It has mastered the sins of all its relatives: carrion eater, pilferer and nest-robber. Like all pied things, it has a jester's notoriety: it looks like a fool, yet is too wise for its own good. It is superfluous to quote the plethora of rhymes which find omens in the number of magpies that cross one's path; they are at once too ubiquitous and too variable. More interesting is the other feature of the magpie-meeting ritual: the respectful tipping of the hat, tugging of the collar or pulling of the forelock, the addressing of the magpie as "Sir" or "Mister", and the enquiry after the health of his wife. Here is a living tradition, still practised across Britain, in which an act of propitiation, often openly admitted to be superstitious, is in fact made with a certain degree of awe and trepidation. We have evidence, too, of other magpie-traditions which were still very much alive in the nineteenth century. A dream-book, written in around 1880 by "Zadkiel", explains that: "To dream that you see a magpie, foretells that you will soon be married, but that you will lose your partner in a few years after your union. To dream you see two magpies, it denotes that you will be married twice, and be twice widowed. And if a man dreams that he sees three magpies, it portends the death of his wife in childbed, and also the death of the child."

Sibly, whose notes on fortune-telling were printed in the same book, had some sage advice for young ladies confounded by the receipt of anonymous valentines. To reveal the author, you must "prick the fourth finger of your left hand, and with a crow-quill write on the back of the valentine the day, hour and year of your birth...Try this on the first Friday after you receive the valentine, but do not go to bed till midnight; place the paper in your left shoe, and put it under your pillow, lay on your left side..." My imagination is at it again: she sits, slightly dizzy from a too-tight corset, dizzier still from the heady thought of a gentleman's infatuation, blushing, perhaps, at the thought of it – and then works witchcraft so potent that one wonders whether she is all that different from the modern teen-witch who drinks diet coke and invokes Black Shuck: the pricked finger, the left hand, the writing in blood. And she uses a magical item which is as common as dirt, yet more powerful than any number of crystal-tipped wands: the feather of a

The Curse of the Oracle: Corvids in Myth & Lore

crow. When she dreams, I wonder will she, as she wishes, see the face of her lover? Or will she see the spirit of Badhbh, taking flight towards the "rooky wood", before her eyes are blinded by upturned soil?

Chapter Five

Yaffles, Gabble-Ratchets, Wudu-Snites and Assilags

We called it the Baba Yaga's house, although it was not on stilts of hens' legs, nor surrounded by human bones. The windows were long boarded up, the dark-stained, deep-carved timber framework spanned by spiders' webs. An eight-foot fence bounded it on two sides, topped with taut barbed wire. Yellow notices warned of marauding dogs. Beyond it, tangled briars and elders formed an impenetrable screen, and beyond those again, a mile or more of beechwood whispered in the wind. We lived opposite, in a little thatched cottage in the grounds of a school, and watched the blue-tits raising their broods, the dunnocks grubbing amongst the blackberries, and the bullfinches, in the full blaze of their pomposity, perching upon the thorn. At dusk, strange sounds came from the woods: in the deadest cold of winter, foxes coughed their lungs out, and owls held hallowed conversations in the glowing gloom. In summer, other, haunting noises emerged from behind Baba Yaga's house, an assortment of pics and yaffles, and in the daytime, deep hollow rattles, like the knocking of aged ghosts on locked doors. The authors of these chthonic noises were elusive, but at last they came into the garden, looping between the boughs with a loping flight, landing vertically on the trunk of the old apple tree in the centre of the lawn. They were woodpeckers, pied and red-smocked, with faces painted like skulls. They gathered nuts and faded back into the leaves, while their green and blood-capped cousins plied the lawn for worms, or licked the ants into minor oblivions.

The drumming of a woodpecker is reminiscent of rain and thunder. The sound is achieved by pounding a branch with the bill-tip at a frequency of five to twenty strikes per half-second; the base of a woodpecker's beak is padded with shock-absorbent tissue to prevent its brain being mashed by the inertia. The great folklorist and ornithologist Edward Armstrong maintained that a woodpecker cult arose in this country and across Europe during Neolithic times, when the earliest attempts at farming increased the rain-dependence of human societies. There is evidence to suggest that there was a woodpecker oracle in the Apennines, who divined the weather. It is easy to see how the earliest agriculturalists could have worshipped these birds, calling upon them to bring the thrumming of the rain, as the oak boles rattled, probed by the tongue of the Woodwale. Into the Bronze Age the Hew Hole held her own, but the oak forests diminished, and Zeus ousted the cult of the Awl Bird. The woodpeckers, vilified by believers in the gods, became mere birds once again. A speech by Euripedes, in Aristophanes' Birds explains:

> *Zeus won't in a hurry the sceptre restore to the woodpecker tapping the oak,*
> *In times prehistoric 'tis easily proved, by evidence weighty and ample, That birds and not gods were rulers of men, and the lords of the world.*

Other state religions drubbed the woodpecker too for good measure: always, she was disobedient to some male god, refusing to dig holes in the earth for him on the grounds that it would ruin her impeccable plumage. In North Wales, it was said that Christ one day turned an old woman into a woodpecker for refusing him food and water, assuming, of course, that she had any to offer. On those long summer evenings, however, with a full moon rising, and the woodpeckers jostling in the green, it was easy for me to ignore all those pipsqueak interventions of institutionalised gods. The woodpeckers ruled the weather, and the weather ruled the world.

A near relative of these woodpeckers, the bark-coloured wryneck, is a bird of primeval magical power. Ancient Greeks and Romans tied the living bird to a wheel known as an Iynx, its wings outspread, and spun it to aid in the wooing process, or to bring back strays with their tails between their legs. The witch Iyinx herself cast a love-spell on Zeus, leading him into infidelity with Io, and was turned into a wryneck for her pains. The bird's generic name, Jynx, comes from this, and the name for the malefic use of the wryneck has since come to be applied to any spell designed to hobble or cripple an enemy. As John Clare observed, nest-robbing attempts by unruly schoolboys nearly always failed when the prospective victim was a wryneck, for the bird would cling steadfastly to the nest, writhing and hissing with its neck awry, its crest erect, its eagle-eyes staring. The ability of the bird to twist its neck like a throttled snake has given it the specific name *torquilla*, or 'little twister', and it bears the magical power of all crooked things. It is a boon to the jealous lover who cares not for the consequences, who pronounces the witch-bird's jinx upon the foe, the rival in love, whose jibe shall choke upon his tongue as the bird's eye glares upon him.

Earthier still is the lore surrounding nightjars, also known as Fern Owls for their habit of hiding amongst the bracken,

Yaffles, Gabble-Ratchets, Wudu-Snites & Assilags

as Razor Grinders for their night-time churr which makes them reminiscent of great-eyed crickets, as Dor Hawks for their habit of catching moths on the wing, and more obscurely, as Gabble Ratchets. They share the latter name with the Gabriel Hounds of the Wild Hunt, and their status as faerie birds is guaranteed as much by their secretive habits and cryptic appearance as it is by the folklore which surrounds them. At Nidderdale, it has long been believed that the souls of unbaptised infants go into Nightjars as they go flitting wide-mouthed in the gloom, moth-catching in moonglow. There is also a long-established and highly libellous superstition which maintains that at night-time, the Nightjars go muffle-feathered to the goat-yard, their puckish beaks agape, and drain and poison the udders of she-goats, causing the teats to shrivel, and the goats to dodder and die. It is easy to make an imaginative leap which unites the two traditions in a hideous, vampiric-gothic fantasy, in which the Lich-Fowl (another of their multitudinous names) fly moth-winged to the unhallowed borders of the churchyard, jaws ajar, dripping milk and blood upon their own graves.

Goldcrests and Short-Eared Owls are believed to be the pilots of the Wudu-Coc, Wudu-Snite or Woodcock, because they are migrants who arrive in Britain slightly earlier. Tradition holds that the Woodcock themselves all arrive in Britain overnight, close to Samhain, and it is certainly true that most of them are here by then. Stranger by far is the belief, allied perhaps to the pre-nineteenth century insistence that swallows hibernated under lakes and ponds, that the Woodcocks in their time of absence have migrated to the dark side of the moon. It was Olaus Magnus who first proposed, in the sixteenth century, the more prosaic notion that these species were involved in more-or-less earthbound migratory patterns, but he was not believed, and the mystical flight of the Wudu-Coc to and from the moon was an accepted fact of natural history until well into the eighteenth century. The woodcock has also been used in weather-augury; it is maintained that the early arrival of the woodcock is a good omen for farmers, whereas its late arrival signals disaster, as does a failure to gather the hay before its arrival. Like the Nightjar, the Woodcock seems to conform to the law that the more secretive the bird, the more esoteric its significance.

The mystique of bird lore is just as compelling in the rarefied lives of lighthouse-keepers and fisherfolk. The Assilag, or Storm Petrel, will serve as an example. The very existence of the bird is seemingly miraculous, for it survives the full force of Atlantic gales in a body the size of a sparrow. Its elements may be air and water, but the stuff of life for the petrel is oil; its body oozes with the stuff. Occasionally, they find themselves shipwrecked, whirled inland, and human beings may pick them up alive on the beach. A portion of their bowel contents are reserved just for the occasion, for a rescued petrel will instantly mute black oil on its perceived attacker. For this reason, it has also been called Oily Mootie. In fact, the bird's body is so heavily bathed in oil that lighthouse keepers have been known to run string through their bodies and use them as candles; an example of a bird prepared in such a way may be seen in the Pitt Rivers Museum in Oxford. Storm Petrels are widely held to embody the damned souls of sailors, especially those of cruel or unjust skippers, which perhaps accounts for the callous detachment with which they are turned into candles. That they are harbingers not only of bad weather, but of evil, was long undisputed. Two further folk names for these birds are suggestive of supernatural associations: Waterwitch, and Mother Carey's Chicken. The latter is the subject of much dispute amongst folklorists. Was Mother Carey a corruption of Mother Mary, making the name an invocation of a goddess, half-assimilated by Christianity, for the protection of sailors? Or was Mother Carey herself a witch who, like the North Berwick witches who reputedly tried to assassinate King James by magical means, was implicated in the sinking of some ship? Once again, the sources of the names, and the legends that lie behind them, are as elusive as the bird itself.

Other birds have reputations equally charged with lore. The barnacle goose is so-named because Gerald of Wales and the medieval bestiarists claimed that it had a metamorphic life-cycle, spending the first half of its life in the form of goose barnacles. Gerard the herbalist, normally so rational, claimed to have verified this by his own observations. Oystercatchers are traditionally Bride's birds, which she carries under her crooked arms and releases as she brings the spring to Celtic countries. The body-weight of herons is said to wax and wane with the moon. Ovid believed that kingfishers made nests of fishbone on the sea. The Barn Owl is the descendent of Blodeuwedd, the maiden composed of flowers from the *Mabinogion*, who was turned into an owl for committing adultery and attempted murder. When curlews fly in flocks of seven, they are to be feared, because they are the incarnation of the Seven Whistlers, and harbingers of doom. Their folk-name Whaup aligns them with a Scottish goblin of the same name, and their bills are suitably downturned for snatching souls. Non-passerine birds in particular are often the focus of our most elemental fears. Their reputations are suffused with some of the most ancient forms of magic: auguries, love-charms and shape-shifting. Whatever twitchers may tell you, it is a crime to be mawkish about birds, and still more so to tick them off on a list. Any fossil of *Archaeopteryx* will show you why – the scaled legs, the flattened eyes, the additional neck vertebrae all attest to it – birds are dinosaurs writ small, disguised with quills and down.

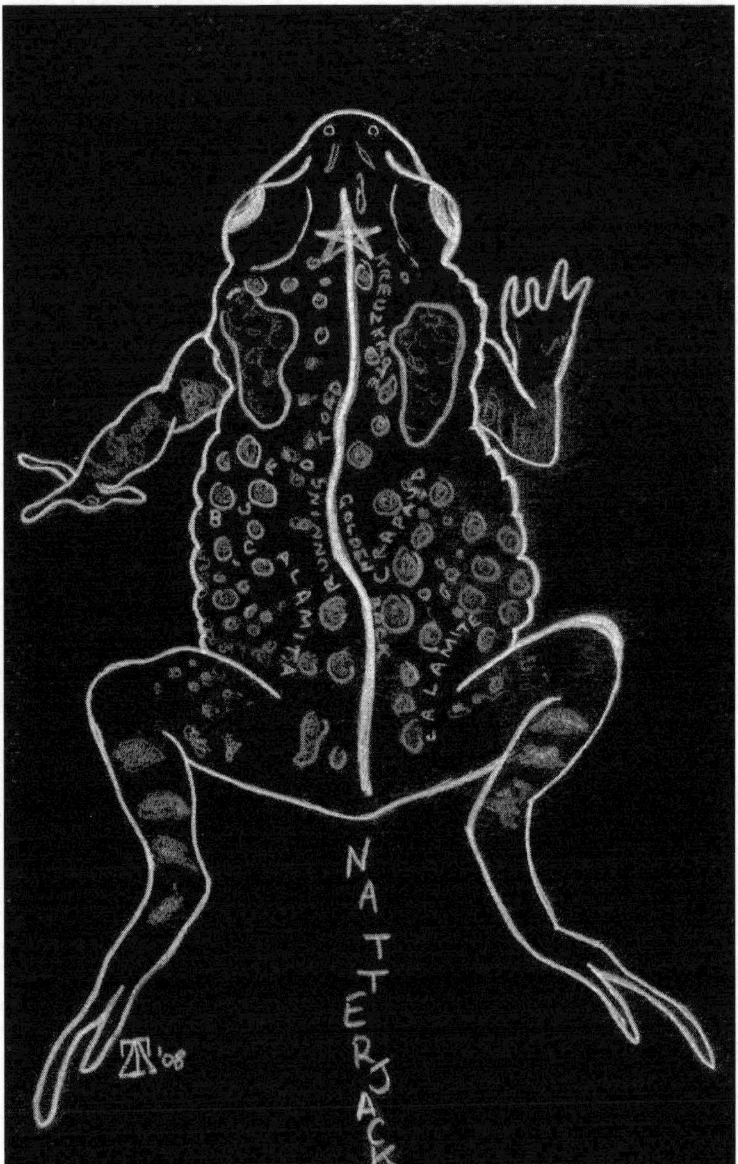
RUNNING TOAD
NATTERJACK

Chapter Six

'Foul and Loathsome Animals': Amphibians and the Lore of the Witch

"Amphibians are abhorrent: their bodies corpse-cold, pale of pigment, gristly of skeleton, squalid of skin, malign of eye, offensive of stench, vulgar of voice, horrendous of habitation, lethal of venom; so the Deity disdained manufacturing too many of them."

So wrote the influential biological taxonomist Carl Linnaeus, originator of the binomial system of classification by Latin names, in his *Systema Naturae* of 1766. It is perhaps unfortunate for the reputations of the amphibians that Linnaeus was raised in Sweden. It is a trick of evolution that adverse conditions produce greater diversity: in northern Europe, where there is plenty of rainfall, conditions are ideal for frogs, toads and newts, and yet there are only a handful of species. In the semi-arid zones of Australia, where I grew up, there are more than a hundred species of frog, and in the eyes of a small boy, none of them were abhorrent. A favourite was the Pobblebonk, a squat, brown creature which inhabited sphagnum bogs, hiding well under the moss in order to evade the tiger snakes. It earned its name because of its call, which consisted of a series of deep, sporadic and randomly spaced *bonks*. I would spend hours turning over logs in the dry sclerophyll forest at the feet of the Brindabella mountains, in search of the Corroboree Frog, so named because its dorsal side is a pattern of bright yellow and black stripes, reminiscent of the ritual body paint used by Aboriginal tribesmen. Turn the creature over on its back, and a glistening belly is revealed, in all the colours of polished marble. The variety is seemingly unending: there are burrowing frogs which hide under the desert sands throughout the dry season, and live like embryos enveloped in membranes as watery as amniotic sacs; there are vivid green tree frogs with suckers on their feet, and frogs whose nuptial orgies rival any dawn chorus for melodious virtuosity. In Queensland, there is the notorious introduced Cane Toad - the skin of its back blistered with great, swollen poison glands - whose numbers reach plague proportions, and whose baleful glandular secretions are reportedly combined with puffer-fish poison to produce zombie slaves in Haiti. Newspapers occasionally report the discovery of outrageously obese specimens the size of footballs. In Britain, however, the diversity is more limited: there are only three species of newt, two species of toad, and one frog native to these islands. Yet the folklore associated with these six species is perhaps richer than anywhere else in the world, and most of this is inspired by our two species of toad, whose association with witches is nothing short of symbiotic.

This symbiosis is evident both in the iconography of the witches' sabbat, and in the confessions of persecuted witches throughout Europe. In Gustave Doré's inspiring and energetic engraving of *Le Ronde du Sabbat* (1870), the horned one holds torches aloft in the darkness as he stands upon a stone altar. At his feet, a witch is seated, her wand upraised, and about them whirls a dance: naked women whisk by, alongside men with bats' wings, cockerels' heads and other composite forms. Bats fly into the night, and in the background, a corpse hangs from a gallows: one of the martyred witches, perhaps, or a dead man whose dying ejaculation will engender a mandrake. In the foreground of all this frenzied, kinetic, and irrepressibly joyful action, there are two mute spectators: a toad and a snake. In Louis Breton's engraving, *The He-Goat Opens the Sabbath* (1863), two witches and the goat are cavorting with similar energy, but on this occasion, again in the foreground, the toad joins in, prancing on his hind legs with his forelimbs waving gracefully in the half-light. Such depictions are not merely the product of nineteenth century romanticism. A toad demon figures prominently in an engraving of the phantasms of a shaman's ecstasy in the works of Olaus Magnus (1555), and in an English pamphlet depicting the hangings of the Chelmsford witches in 1589, Joan Prentice is shown in the company of three toad familiars, two of whom are mating underneath the gallows.

When the seventy-year-old widow Dame Julian Cox was tried for witchcraft in Taunton in 1663, a witness insisted that her toad familiar had persistently pestered him after she invited him to join her in smoking tobacco from clay pipes. As he was lighting up, the toad, attracted by the warmth of his crotch, raised its head from between his legs. "What a pretty thing there is!" remarked Dame Julian, pointing to it, but he begged to disagree, casting down the pipe and stabbing at the toad with his walking stick before hurrying off to his home some two miles away. Perhaps the toad was grieved to see its mistress snubbed, for that night as he sat stuffing his own pipe at home, the toad emerged once more from between his thighs. The distracted smoker picked the toad up by one toe and hurled it to the floor, but when he settled down to his pipe once more, it quickly returned. Perhaps this time it licked the buttons of his fly, for he flew into a rage, took up his paring knife, and sliced the toad into strips. Within minutes, the toad had recovered from its dismemberment, and made its way up the folds of his britches, so he took it in his fist and hurled it in the fire, but still it reconstituted itself and returned. He took up a switch and thrashed the poor, persevering toad out of the house, whereupon the creature vanished, although it is safe to assume that the man's taste for tobacco was much impaired thereafter.

There are many similar accounts of witches entertaining toad familiars. Elizabeth Stile, or one of her confederates, tried in 1579, is depicted in a pamphlet feeding toads with a spoon. Margery Sammon's mother (1582) gave her a gift of some toads in a wicker basket, and told her, "If thou dost not give them milk, they will suck of thy blood." Joan Upney's daughter (1589) was very kind to toads although her sister despised them. Charles I's physician Dr Harvey claimed to have discredited the magical powers of a Newmarket witch by eviscerating her toad with a dissecting knife; a callous act indeed given that the woman was so fond of the creature that she fed it with milk from her own breast. An Essex witch with the picturesque name of Joan Cunny (1589) was in the habit of kneeling in obeisance to her two familiars, which took the form of black frogs, or of black dogs "faced like a toad". Mediaeval bestiaries had insisted that "frogs signify the heretics and their demons who linger at the banquet of the decadent senses". By 1572, the writings of Zurich pastor Ludwig Lavater suggest that Catholic and Protestant demonologists had reached an agreement that spirits which took the form of toads were invariably evil, in contrast to those which materialised in the form of doves or lambs, which might be angels in disguise. In the early seventeenth century, the witches of Labourd in the Pyrenees often danced with toads – one well-to-do lady cavorted with no less than four at once – and their children, who were not quite ready for some of the more flagrant excesses of the full sabbatic rite, were equipped with white twigs and sent off to the side of a stream, where they shepherded the toads at pasture (indeed, witches' children are depicted doing precisely this in one corner of Jan Ziarnko's engraving of *Du Sabbat des Sorciers*, an illustration for the inquisitor Pierre de Lancre's own racy account of goings on at Labourd). At the last witch-burning in Labourd, "a multitude" of toads were said to have escaped from the head of the victim. The Basque witches, persecuted by the Spanish Inquisition, liked to dress their toads in cowls. Back in Britain, by the time of Isobel Gowdie's confession in 1662, the tales of witches' associations with their toad familiars had grown more elaborate, for she and her confederates had spellbound a farmer's field by circumnavigating it with a tiny model plough yoked with toads.

Nearly all of these examples associate the toad with womanhood, and the perceived ugliness of the toad may explain this connection. The warty texture of a toad's skin allies it with the image of the crone. More importantly, whether the toad is supremely beautiful or supremely ugly is a thoroughly subjective matter. All of us have encountered mothers – and fathers too - who are convinced that their newborn offspring is the most beautiful human being alive, whilst the rest of the world, quietly realistic, affirms that the child looks like a withered prune. Witches who suckle toads at their breasts might be seen as similarly deluded, but their delusion is in fact enlightenment, and we spurn the toad at our own expense: a fact which is recognised by the authors of European fairy tales, whose toads are always princes, as it is in the Russian folk tradition, where the amphibian may just as likely transform into a ravishingly beautiful Tsarevna with magical powers. Whilst Milton places Satan "Squat like a Toad, close at the ear of Eve", Hieronymus Bosch covers a woman's genitals with a toad rather than a fig leaf as a warning against sexual temptation, and Spenser makes Envy ride on the back of a wolf whilst chewing on a toad, it has also been said that the man who would kill a toad would just as lightly kill his own mother. Indeed, it is a pity Dr Harvey did not pause to consider this proverb. Perhaps he listened too much to tales of Fair Rosamond, whom Queen Eleanor was said to have dispatched by getting an old hag to attach her toad familiars to the damsel's breasts, whereupon they sucked her blood to the last drop.

One entirely masculine magical tradition explicitly recommends the killing of a toad. The survival of the "toad bone amulet" as a magical tool from antiquity to the present day, and its gradual transformation into a self-initiatory witchcraft ritual involving the devil in the nineteenth century, is the subject of an article by Andrew Chumbley which is essential reading for anyone interested in the interface between folklore, witchcraft and natural history. The amulet, initially consisting of two bones, and later of one, was variously employed throughout history as a love charm, a means of controlling animals and changing water temperature, a prophylactic against disease, and a token of diabolic initiation. By the end of this process, the toadmen of Wisbech in Cambridgeshire observed an elaborate initiation ritual. A live toad was captured and skinned alive, or pegged to an ant-heap until the flesh was eaten. The toad's bones were then carried in the initiate's pocket until dry (the eighteenth century wise woman Tilly Baldry preferred to deposit the live toad in her bosom until it was thoroughly decomposed), whereupon they would be cast into a stream. One bone would detach itself from the others, sometimes, like the uprooted mandrake, emitting a fearful scream; this bone would be retrieved, and would be the new toadman's source of magical power. For three nights in a row, the toadman would carry his toad bone amulet into a stable, and on the last night, the Devil would appear, and initiate him by drawing his blood. In some variants, the Devil would fight the initiate for the bones, or even try to snatch the bones away at the stream. Quasi-masonic guilds such as the Horseman's Word in Scotland, as well as the solitary East Anglian practitioners, excelled in horse-whispering after conducting the ritual, and could unerringly stop a horse in its tracks.

Perhaps the ability of the amulet to confer power over animals implies an element of sympathetic magic, for when threatened, a toad will inflate its lungs and assume a statuesque defence position, with head tucked downwards and legs extended to their full length. Older natural history textbooks include pictures of toads which have adopted this position after being thrown alive into formalin or preserving alcohol; it is a moot point whether the authors of these books would have considered murdering their own mothers. In any case, to move from the sublime to the ridiculous, the role of the real toad as victim of the ignorant is doubtless preserved in folk-tales of the tick-toad, recorded in Darlaston, Staffordshire and in Bishop's Cannings, Wiltshire. The reaction of the yokels who find the tick-toad is always the same: smash it to pieces with whatever piece of agricultural equipment is nearest to hand. Always, they are blissfully unaware that the tick-toad is merely a pocket-watch, inadvertently left behind by some wayfaring gentleman.

Why have such lowly creatures inspired such a wealth of folklore? The answer surely lies in their natural history. The very word "amphibian" is a clue to their magical significance: the toad and its relatives are equally at home on earth and in water, making them liminal, trans-elemental creatures, like fairies. In Aristophanes' delightful comedy, it is the frogs, rather than Charon, who are the most vocal guardians of the Styx, for "If it came on to rain/ We'd dive under again/ (To avoid getting soaked)/ And still harder we croaked/ From under the slime/ Our subaqueous rhyme/... And burst with a plop at the top,/ Breplep!" Ancient Egyptians must have noticed the abundance of frogs in the places where they collected moist clay for their pottery; perhaps this is why they worshipped a frog-headed goddess of childbirth called Heket, whose name perhaps echoes the noise made by the frogs themselves. Toads have long been said to be capable of remaining alive when encased in solid stone. One John Malpas, for example, informed the *Gentleman's Magazine* in 1756 that he had found an adult toad whilst dividing a piece of solid free-stone: "I took the toad out of the hole with my compass; I did not observe that I in any ways hurt it... [but] when it was on the ground it hopped about, and died in less than one hour." A further example, encased in a nodule of flint, is on display in the Booth Museum in Brighton. There is something magical, too, about the tongues of amphibians, which are rooted to the front rather than the back of the mouth, allowing an almost mystical proficiency for catching flies. The sinister hag in Ben Jonson's *Masque of Queens* (1609) surely recognised this when she used the skin of a frog as a purse, in which she imprisoned a crane-fly: "The blood of frog and bone in his back/ I have been getting and made of his skin/ A purset to keep Sir Cranion in."

The metamorphic life-history of amphibians (as well as their ability to change colour in different environments) is also suggestive of shape-shifting, and is all the more magically potent because the tadpole appears to "breathe" one alchemical element – water – through its gills, whereas adult amphibians clearly have lungs and breathe air. The metamorphosis also effectively turns the toad in particular into an "earthy" creature which only returns to the water to breed. It is little wonder that some classical enthusiast for all things amphibian thought it would be satisfying to associate the salamander with fire, thereby spawning a string of fantastic accounts in mediaeval bestiaries. Perhaps the insistence of Pliny and Agrippa that certain toad bones had the power to either stop water from boiling, or to increase its temperature, is another way of making toads the masters of all the alchemical elements. The importance of metamorphosis is oddly emphasised by the ability of some amphibians, notably newts and salamanders, to attain their full reproductive capabilities whilst still in the larval stage. Richard Dawkins, who has more recently been sidetracked into a futile assault on fundamentalist religion, once made the attractive suggestion that we humans relate to this amphibian tendency – technically known as neoteny – because we too, with our hairless bodies, are like apes who have somehow never grown up. Perhaps this explains the vogue in the 1970s for keeping neotenous axolotls as pets.

The extraordinary ability of frogs to entirely fill a garden pond with their spawn has made them symbols of fertility: another persuasive magical credential. Like us, all amphibians are bilaterally symmetrical on the outsides of their bodies, but the dorsal surface of a natterjack toad is divided by a yellow vertebral stripe which is never quite straight – a hint, perhaps, of the creature's crooked nature. Moreover, captive amphibians frequently exhibit behavioural characteristics which we instinctively associate with intelligence – not least amongst these is the tendency of frogs and toads to exhibit resentment. Place two toads in a fish-tank with an unsuspecting fly. The first toad to catch the fly will most likely be snapped at by its haughty companion. Finally, something about the bodily simplicity of batracians is, to us, grotesque, and therefore inherently magical. If a toad eats something unpleasant, it must vomit up its entire stomach and then swallow it again. The oesophagus of an amphibian is not equipped with the muscles required for peristalsis: the morsel, whether blowfly, cranion, or in some extraordinary cases, a full-grown mouse, is forced further down the digestive system by the pressure of the creature's eyeballs, which are able to be depressed right through the skull. Indeed, the average toad appears to practise this reflex at regular intervals, whether or not an insect is lodged in the gullet: readers who do not wish to confirm this by observation in the flesh can do so by tracking Touchwood through episodes of *Catweazle* on DVD.

Dog owners may have observed that their pets have a marked aversion to toads, for any dog which seizes a toad will rapidly exhibit symptoms of extreme distress, and begin to foam at the mouth. Hedgehogs have been observed to make use of toads in a similar manner when they wish to produce a surfeit of frothy saliva for their own bizarre self-anointing rituals. Toads exude a complex cocktail of biotoxins from their cutaneous glands, including bufotalin and bufogin, which act upon the central nervous system, and slow the heart to an alarming degree. A person who ate a toad would fare little better than a person who had feasted on a salad of foxgloves, for the effect of these toxins is rather similar to that of digitalis: a fact well understood by Roman women who wished to be rid of their husbands. Indeed, natural selection has at times weeded out misguided members of the human race who have mistaken members of the genus *Bufo* for edible frogs. Unfortunately it has also weeded out some innocent French witches, who in 1390 were blamed along with the Jews for poisoning wells with toads' blood. Additional side-effects of toad secretions include muscular paralysis and irritation of the mucus membranes. The alkaloid bufotenine is also hallucinogenic. This fact alone has contributed to the toad's mystical credentials, and perhaps promoted the cultural association between toads and poisonous mushrooms - or toadstools - which is common both to Europeans and to the Mayans of

Mesoamerica. The skin of all amphibians tastes disgusting; even newts, which the stalwart herpetologist Miss Ormerod tasted in 1892, give out an "acrid exudation": "The first effect was a bitter astringent feel in the mouth, with irritation of the upper part of the throat, numbing of the teeth... and in about a minute a strong flow of clear saliva. This was accompanied by much foam and violent spasmodic action..." The admirable Miss Ormerod also noted that an alarmed newt emitted an odour of "bruised poppy-heads" – an allusion which suggests she was a woman of wide experience, and perhaps one who would have been a candidate for denunciation to the Inquisition in an earlier century. Today she might be subject to surveillance by a narcotics squad. In any case, throughout the centuries, witches have learnt much about defence strategies from their amphibian friends.

As old age advances, it lies within the power of the witch to retain a certain charisma whilst acquiring all of the characteristics of the archetypal hag. So it is with amphibians; just try staring into the eye of a toad. The iris is the most gorgeous dream wrought in gold, as Shakespeare's Juliet affirmed: "Some say the lark and the loathed toad change eyes." Some say that the beauty of the toad's eye is the source of the myth that it carries a precious jewel embedded in its skull, although it is more likely that the jewel was originally simply the bone sought by mediaeval magicians and the toadmen of East Anglia alike. A toad's voice may be beguiling too; W.H Hudson, in a delightful turn of phrase, likened it to a "fairy bassoon". The toad's power of beguiling is no better attested than by the eighteenth century naturalist Thomas Pennant, who described it as "The most deformed and hideous of all animals... its general appearance is such as to strike one with disgust and horror." Yet he tenderly kept a tame old lady toad under his doorstep for thirty-six years. Daily, the toad hurried to greet his scab-kneed children, or sat on the kitchen table, ready to be regaled with earthworms. Doubtless Pennant watched the loving way she wrapped her tongue around her writhing prey, and once or twice he saw her lap up her own nutritious skin, wriggling free from the back end of it with the fore-part down her throat. Perhaps he watched her toes twitch with anticipation, her lovely eyes tracking a fly, and suddenly the squat lady toad would be transformed into a leaping dream, a keen-tongued hunter: lark-eyed but unlovely, reviled and yet revered. It is no wonder that the toad has become the archetypal witch's familiar: seemingly a land animal, yet born of water; seemingly vulnerable, yet possessing an almost impregnable battery of defence mechanisms; seemingly ugly, yet beautiful on closer inspection; seemingly clumsy, yet agile enough to transfix a fly without stirring a limb. We witches cannot help but have an affinity with toads. A cursory glance from the uninitiated will never penetrate the skin.

Chapter Seven

'Adder's Fork and Blind-Worm's Sting': the Magical Reptile

It was one of those romantic and magical moments which, as one discovers later, it is impossible quite to replicate – but fear not. The cliché will have been subverted by the end of this paragraph. We had spent a blissful, mutually indulgent weekend in a thatched coaching inn, somewhere near to the heart of the Cotswolds. It was sunny beyond expectation, so we walked to the next village, admiring the crazy-eyed chickens which stood, cock-headed on a stone wall, as though expecting something importune, like the hatching of a Cockatrice. We poked around the church, shadowed at every window by suitably pagan yews, and then walked on by some bucolic alley which promised nothing in particular – only an idyll. At one side of it there was a stream, and at the other, another of those Cotswold walls, embedded in an earthen bank. The path led to an archetypal cottage of rough-hewn stone; wicker archways and roses in the garden. Ivy thrust wormlike roots through the crevices in the stone wall, creating dappled arbours suitable for those who dwelt within. This first warm day of spring, they were sluggish, absorbing the rays of the low sun, slow moving with a constant hiss, sliding viscerally through gaps in the stones. There was only one way to approach them: bare-footed, respectful, with wonder, and not fear. The adjoining stream was evidently their larder: here, frogs would conglomerate to mate, oozing frogspawn. The grass snakes would catch them by their toes, and gulp them down alive, so that the croak could still be heard within the gaping gullets. The struggle would continue awhile, within their guts. Later in the year, the grass snakes would feast on tadpoles, diving in the bubbling gushes, and gobbling them on lush grass. Their skins grown old, they would slide through twigs to slough them, their eyes glazed. The snakes live there to this day. We go back to see them sometimes, just for the sake of it.

You may have had any of a number of reactions to the paragraph above. It may have incited fear or disgust; if so, I pity you, and there is little more to be said. Indeed, I am surprised you started reading at all. Or perhaps you will opt for the Freudian interpretation: snakes have no limbs, and the more advanced species do not even possess pelvic girdles – hence they are phallic. Watson wasn't being romantic at all – he was blinded by his lust, which he was hoping to satisfy behind the hedgerow around the corner. I fear that Freudians are secularised Christians who see a serpent coiled around every tree, and the fruit of the tree of knowledge of good and evil is filled with semen. This is to oversimplify snakes, just as it is to over-exaggerate the difference between *eros* and *agape*. The real reason why snakes are intensely romantic creatures for me is that they are entwined with my past; my memories, including the one I have just recalled are all lovingly wrapped in serpentine coils.

Growing up in south-eastern Australia, my first encounters with snakes were characterised by one emotion alone: awe. The first snake I remember encountering (I might have been five) was a red-bellied black snake swimming across a pond. As it emerged, my father turned it gently with his walking stick, and the scales on the underside were like a streak of undulating blood in the tussocky grass. It was not stupendously venomous by Australian standards, but well enough equipped to kill a small child. I remember when an expert herpetologist visited our school, commanding our obedient silence as he milked a sinuous taipan, its venom drooling into a plastic phial as he pinched it behind the jaw. It produces more venom than any other snake in the world; enough to make any health and safety legislator blue in the face. My first death adder was encountered on the road to Forbes, the town in the semi-arid zone of New South Wales which was the centre for the daring exploits of the bushranger Ben Hall – a man who must have met innumerable snakes before his life terminated at the end of a rope. It lay flaccid at the side of the road, seemingly too fat to form coils, and too torpid to move as I crouched to photograph it, half camouflaged against the rust-red earth.

The poison glands in its head could have killed ten children of my body mass, and then could have killed ten more, as fast as a man can moisten his mouth after he has spat himself dry. And then there was that delicious moment when I was a teenage volunteer at the R.S.P.C.A, and a worried-looking family brought something bulging like blancmange inside a pillow case. I took one look inside, let out a shout of triumph, and delved within, my arms entwined with loving twists of diamond python. Once, years later, I was wearing him around my neck when I answered the door to some Jehovah's Witnesses: a more effective repellent of intinerant evangelists has never been discovered.

Britain has three snake species, and among these, only one is venomous, albeit comparatively mildly so. In common with that of rattlesnakes and other forms of viper, Adder venom is primarily a haemotoxin, attacking the red blood cells and causing haemorrhage, in contrast to the neurotoxic venom of elapid snakes. Adder bites rarely cause human deaths unless they have not bitten for some time, or unless the victim is already infirm, or very young, but these have been enough to gain the snake both notoriety and folkloric significance. Thomas Hardy's *Return of the Native* incidentally records much of this folklore when Clym Yeobright finds his mother lying in the furze with an injured foot: "It was swollen and red. Even as they watched, the red began to assume a more livid colour, in the midst of which appeared a scarlet speck, smaller than a pea, which was found to consist of a drop of blood, which rose above the smooth flesh of her ankle in a hemisphere." The immediate diagnosis, "She has been stung by an adder", reflects the old country belief that the adder "stings" with its tongue. An adder's fangs hinge backwards when not in use, and so are not immediately obvious in dead specimens, so that the "adder's fork" used by the witches in *Macbeth*

'Adder's Fork & Blind-Worm's Sting': the Magical Reptile

was long considered to be the origin of the poison. (Oddly, the Adder's tongue fern, which was considered efficacious in the treatment of snakebites, is not forked at all, and the "blind worm" or slow worm, whose "sting" they also throw into the cauldron, is in fact a harmless, legless lizard.) Yeobright's acquaintance Sam tells him, "There is only one way to cure it. You must rub the place with the fat of other adders, and the only way to get that is by frying them." Sam accordingly goes out with his lantern, and returns with three adders hanging from his walking stick. Two of them are already dead, for – tellingly – he has killed them earlier that day whilst at work furze-cutting, and the third is still alive, for the fat is, apparently, only efficacious when fried from an adder which has just been killed. However, Sam is well-versed in adder lore, for he knows that the fat of the dead ones may still be potent: "as they don't die till the sun goes down they can't be very stale meat". The assumption that adders cannot die until sunset is no doubt a reflection of the snake's resilience, for a mortally wounded adder will often writhe and make its escape, dying some hours later. Another onlooker at Mrs Yeobright's bedside, Christian Cantle, thinks that the serpent of the Garden of Eden lives on in the adder, and cries, "Look at his eye – for all the world like a villainous sort of black currant. 'Tis to be hoped he can't ill wish us! There's folks on the heath who've been overlooked already. I will never kill another adder as long as I live." In fact, whilst the grass snake and the smooth snake both have rounded pupils in their eyes, the adder's pupils are elliptical, narrowing to slits in bright light. Elliptical pupils are normally characteristic of nocturnal creatures such as cats and geckoes, and therefore perhaps more suggestive of the Evil Eye. The three adders are duly chopped and fried, and their fat used to anoint the wound. When the doctor arrives, he affirms that the remedy is recommended by the medical experts, "Hoffman, Mead, and I think the Abbé Fontana", but Mrs Yeobright dies in any case, the poor adder being deemed only partially responsible. Modern adder bites are treated with antihistamines and blood transfusions, although the affected area may also be treated with witch hazel – an update, perhaps, on the viper's bugloss treatment recommended by Dioscorides in the first century.

Other aspects of adder-lore are similarly attributable to the doctrine of signatures: if an adder is poisonous, it must also be medically efficacious. Thus the shed skins of adders are sometimes tied around the forehead to relieve headaches. Further aspects of the folklore are probably inspired by flawed observation. Country folk have often maintained that baby adders will climb into their mother's mouth and hide in her stomach when threatened. As adders bear their young alive, being ovo-viviparous, it is possible that this myth arose when heavily gravid females were killed and cut open to reveal the living young inside. Female adders do also form protective associations with their young, and it has been suggested that the disappearance of the young into the mother's mouth is merely an optical illusion: they are in fact crawling underneath her belly and hiding themselves there whilst the mother's mouth is open in self-defence.

An even older myth concerning the live-bearing adder was first recorded by Herodotus, and survived in a variety of forms into the medieval bestiaries: in the act of mating, the female was supposed to bite off the male's head, only to be repaid in kind by her young, who eat their way out of her body, killing her. According to Pliny the coveted adder-stone of the druids was supposedly obtained when adders congregated and joined their heads together, and somehow extruded the stone encased in bubbles of froth. Adders do indeed meet and join their heads together; the beautiful "dance" of the adders is in fact a ritualised combat between

'Adder's Fork & Blind-Worm's Sting': the Magical Reptile

two males for the possession of a mate, but the snakes do not froth at the mouth. Perhaps the dance of the adders was once observed on a coastal heath, and the cluster of bubbles was a whelk's egg case which chanced to be blown there by the wind – a likely candidate, given that Pliny described the end result as pock-marked and cartilaginous. Another congregation of adders occurs when they entwine themselves together in clumps in order to hibernate. They sometimes remain intertwined when they emerge in spring, making them easy targets for the butt of a gamekeeper's gun: perhaps this, too, gave rise to the idea that the snakes congregated in order to produce the adder-stone.

More difficult to explain is the insistence that adders can kill airborne skylarks by spitting at them and causing them to plummet to the ground; this, one fears, is an example of folklore inspired by pure malice. Never mind. The adder got his own back on human beings long ago, when he caused the battle of Camlann. Both Arthur and Mordred told their men not to charge unless a sword was drawn by the opposing side, but "Ryght so cam out an addir of a lytyll hethe-buysshe, and hit stange a knight in the foote. And so whan the knyght felte hym so stonge, he loked downe and saw the addir; and anone he drew his swerde to sle the addir, and thought none other harme." The rest, of course, is history, or something very like it, and we leave Arthur and Mordred to assail each other with stings of their own. It was not, in any case, the adder's first experience of battle. Hannibal had appreciated the martial potential of venomous snakes long before, and his method was absurdly simple: imprison them en-masse in earthenware jars, shake them up a bit, and throw them at the Romans.

The modern fear of snakes is a degenerate form of the awe with which they were once regarded: an awe which is admirably communicated in D.H. Lawrence's poem, 'Snake',

A Witch's Natural History

in which the serpent is recognised as "one of the lords/ Of life." One of the adder's greatest defenders, W.H. Hudson, suggested that the Judeo-Christian hatred of snakes was a reaction against polytheistic religions which invariably regarded them as sacred. The adder itself was a living mystical sigil, a writhing wyrm whose markings suggest written characters or ogham script. Occasionally one finds an adder whose underside is as plainly marked as the zigzag-patterned dorsal side, and it is said that these markings form the words: "If I could hear as well as see/ No man of life would master me". Snake-handling goddesses are regarded with awe the world over, from the Babylonian Lamashtu, through the Aztec Coatlicue (Lady of the Skirt of Serpents) to the Hindu triple goddess Kali, whose hair was composed of snakes, like that of the Gorgon Medusa. Isis began her career as a snake-goddess – a cobra goddess to be precise – and her most eloquent convert, Apuleius, describes her rising out of the sea with the moon hanging above her forehead, and "Vipers arising from the left-hand and right-hand partings of her hair supported this disc". Hecate carried two snakes, one symbolising healing, and the other sickness and death; perhaps it is her image – or one of her priestesses - that we see in the beautiful Cretan figurine of a woman, bare-breasted in a fashionable bodice and layered skirt, who holds two snakes in her upraised hands. According to Seneca, the much-maligned Medea, another beautiful priestess of Hecate, also bared her breasts and tossed her hair when she handled snakes, and in order to make her potion, which could either heal or kill, she evoked "everything snakelike". It is a pity that her memory has been besmirched by Appolonius of Rhodes, who made her betray her people and the serpent-guardian of the golden fleece to that brazen pirate Jason, and by Euripides, who made her murder her own children in revenge for his subsequent faithlessness. Awe of venomous snakes, combined with a reckless handling of them, was characteristic of the Bacchic and Orphic mysteries immortalised by the murals of Pompeii; indeed, Orpheus's descent into Hades was an attempt to retrieve his beloved, who had been killed by snakebite. Combat with snakes is also invariably imbued with religious significance: the lamentable ophidiophobia of St. George the dragon-slayer, and St. Patrick, who allegedly drove all of the snakes out of Ireland, has a more spiritually significant pedigree in the battle between Apollo and Python, and Thor's wrestlings with the Midgard Serpent – conflicts which perhaps represent the overthrow of female deities by male ones. Even Moses was not averse to a bit of snake shamanism, for it was he who erected the brazen serpent, and following his example, Christian sects such as the Gnostics and the Ophists have depicted Christ crucified as a snake, and consecrated the Eucharist with live serpents. It comes as no surprise that they were soon condemned as heretical, although the caduceus, a serpent entwined around a staff associated with Asclepius, the god of healing, remains to this day a symbol of medicine. Asclepius himself carried two phials of blood from the gorgon Medusa: one to kill, and the other to resurrect – a pagan eucharist indeed.

Perhaps the most beautiful and most subtly erotic snake-myth of all is the story of Cadmus, described in Ovid's *Metamorphoses*. Cadmus once killed a gigantic serpent, and raised an army by sowing its teeth into the soil. Now, he has grown old, and wonders whether the gods are annoyed with him: "If this is what the gods are angry over, may I become a serpent, with a body stretched full-length forward." The words have barely left his lips before he begins to transform. His legs are the first to disappear, and whilst he still possesses arms, he urgently embraces his wife. In her desperation, she pleads with the gods to transform her too, whilst Cadmus, now thoroughly ophidian, glides silkily between her breasts and entwines his body about her neck. She reaches to stroke her serpent husband's scaly skin, and as she does so, she too is transformed, and they make for the woods before the horrified onlookers can beat their brains out or use their vital organs as ancient equivalents to Viagra. Touchingly, Cadmus and is wife are non-venomous; they are indeed "most gentle serpents" who never harm human beings. Perhaps they are pythons, retaining their vestigial pelvic girdles where their legs used to join their bodies. Would that all human beings were given the choice between advancing senility and an eternity as a loving serpent; I know which I would choose. Cleopatra must have been groping towards the same conclusion when she grasped the asp.

In any case, it is the snake's own physiology which is the source of the religious awe it inspires. Anyone who has ever handled a snake knows that it is a creature of exceeding grace and dignity: its scales are smooth as polished jewels, and its undulating mode of locomotion is reminiscent of the movement of flowing water. This fluidity has made it the embodiment of a creator spirit. Even the spirit of Elohim, the creator in the book of Genesis, is first envisaged as moving on the face of the waters, as only a snake can do – an insight which was clearly understood by William Blake when he created his image of a serpent-bodied 'Elohim Creating Adam'. Snakes can dislocate their jaws at will, enabling them to swallow prey which seems impossibly large: a creature which can engulf lesser beings in this way (anacondas have been known to swallow grown men), is bound to be regarded with awe. Snake venom is not only lethal; it also has psycho-active properties, although the reader is advised not to try this at home. It is amazingly durable: a stuffed snake is as venomous as a live one. Male snakes have a double penis, just like the devil, and female

'Adder's Fork & Blind-Worm's Sting': the Magical Reptile

snakes have a paired clitoris – a notion which opens up all sorts of possibilities. A snake discards its skin when it has grown old; it even becomes blind and doddering like a geriatric when the scale which covers the eyeball turns opaque immediately prior to sloughing. It is therefore a metaphor for death and resurrection. When a snake strikes, it often does so with a speed undetectable to the human eye, so it is imbued with mystical power. If one approaches it in the right way, one may handle an adder without retribution – they have indeed been kept as pets by stalwart individuals – but one false move precipitates the lightning strike. Thus snakes are capricious, like the gods. Oviparous snakes like the grass snake, whose young do not hatch in the process of parturition, lay leathern eggs, and there is something mystical about these too; perhaps they, and not the whelk's egg-case, are in fact the *ovum anguinis* of the druids.

Anguis is not, however, the generic name of a snake, but of the lowly slow-worm: not a venomous snake, but a legless lizard. Formerly, it was known as a blind-worm, presumably because its eyes, which have closable lids, are relatively smaller than those of snakes. It is quite harmless, and as its name suggests, rather sluggish in comparison to an adder or smooth snake energised by the sun. Its English relatives, the viviparous and sand lizards, are equally benign, and indeed frequently fall prey to our snakes. It is perhaps more difficult to ascribe magical significance to the *Squamata*, but the Romans seem to have done so, for they sculpted mystical hands out of bronze, with toads, snakes, tortoises and lizards crawling up towards the fingertips. No one knows their significance; perhaps they were fertility or healing charms, or wards against the evil eye. It is noteworthy, perhaps, that all of the animals depicted are cold blooded – but beyond that there is little to be said, save that the hands are clearly objects of power.

On the whole, however, if the snake's biology makes it a likely metaphor for the divine, lizards are clearly earthy and mortal. With some notable warm-weather exceptions, they are not venomous; nor can they dislocate their jaws. They change their skins as snakes do, but slough them in flakes and ribbons rather than slipping them off like gloves. To the uninitiated, they seem altogether prosaic, but any inquisitive crow will tell you a different story. If you would capture a lizard, you must seize it by the head or the body. Grasp it by the tail, and the entire appendage will detach itself by splitting down the middle of one of the vertebrae, whilst the frenzied animal makes its escape through the undergrowth. More perplexing still, the severed tail will continue to undulate and squirm after it has been severed from the spinal column, as energised and frantic as one of Galvin's frog-legs probed with an electrode. Your quarry is safe, and will soon grow a false tail – albeit one without vertebrae – and you have nothing to show for your pains but this threshing bit of scale and bone and gristle. In short, all of the English reptiles are object-lessons for the witch: the grass snake and the smooth snake are her images of occult beauty and erotic power; the adder is her psychopomp and her defense; but the lizard is her most practical guide of all, for he will provide her means of escape should the witch-finder seize her by the tail.

Chapter Eight
The Queen Rat and the Hanoverian Curse

They were the kind of bird-table visitors that only a couple of idiosyncratic witches would welcome. They arrived shortly after the nest-building blue-tits in the early spring, savouring the over-spillings of birdseed and peanuts on the lawn. And as the blue-tit fledglings arrived, so too did their offspring, tottering at first, but daily more confident, and soon as boisterous as strapping adolescent boys. We watched them with delight, and held their increasingly corpulent mother in particular esteem, so much so that we gave her the name of Portia, and soon when we replenished the bird-feeders, we were succumbing to the temptation to spill quantities of seed and nuts upon the ground, just to keep her satisfied. Before long, we were leaving out kitchen scraps too: stale bread, bits of old vegetables, and, on one inspired evening, the skin of a smoked mackerel. Creeping back inside, we watched through the kitchen window, and within half a minute, Portia was out there, her great belly wobbling as she walked, her whiskers aquiver, and her black eyes bulging with anticipation. With a paroxysm of joy, she seized the fish-skin, gave a great leap, clicking her heels in mid-air, and scurried along her well-worn path through the grass to safety. She had looked as happy as the radiant star-jumping youth in William Blake's image of sublime proportion, *Glad Day*. We felt we had witnessed a wildlife spectacle to rival anything narrated by David Attenborough, but few other human beings would have so relished an intimacy with Portia, for she was a representative of that maligned species, *Rattus norvegicus*, known to exterminators, laboratory technicians and pulp-fiction writers alike as the Brown Rat.

Human beings excepted, it is difficult to think of a creature which has conquered the world so completely as the rat, but rats themselves have long been culturally associated with that misunderstood minority amongst humans: witches. Early modern evidence for this association between witches and rats is provided by one of the greatest masterpieces of English literature – and one of its most insidious pieces of propaganda – William Shakespeare's *Macbeth*. *Macbeth* was written for the court of King James I, an obsessive man whose fear of witchcraft was only surpassed by his determination to be rid of his political opponents. His zeal against witchcraft was evident in his alarmingly paranoid treatise on *Daemonologie*, but it also found pragmatic political expression in the expulsion of his estranged cousin Francis, Earl of Bothwell. Bothwell was an occultist, and James had him implicated in a plot with a coven of witches who allegedly tried to assassinate James himself (then James VI of Scotland) in 1590, by raising a storm at sea in an attempt to wreck the king's ship. The 'coven' included a servant girl, Gilly Duncan – the first woman to be compelled to confess – and a cunning woman who perhaps deserves to be regarded as a witch's nearest equivalent to a hero of the faith: the midwife and healer Agnes Sampson. An elderly woman, Sampson was subjected to torture, shaved and searched for the Devil's mark. When this was found in her genitals and she had been "thrawed" with a rope, Sampson confessed to fifty-three charges. These included the use of charms to cause disease, the keeping of a familiar (a well-inhabiting dog called Elva), sailing across the sea to Berwick in a sieve, dancing widdershins, kissing the Devil's buttocks, storm-raising, attempting to poison the king's clothes with the skin secretions of a toad, and making a wax effigy of the king. More than ten years later, Shakespeare reprised Sampson's confession in the dialogue of the three witches on the heath, before their meeting with Macbeth. The witches have two familiars (a toad, Paddock, and a cat, Graymalkin). They plot to raise a storm by sympathetic magic, equipped with the thumb of a drowned pilot, in order to shipwreck a sailor whose wife refused to give the first witch some chestnuts. The first witch vows to go to sea herself in order to ensure that the magic is effective: "in a sieve I'll thither sail,/ And like a rat without a tail, / I'll do, I'll do, and I'll do."

The lowly rat, deprived of her tail as shape-shifted witches so often were, is the first amongst a menagerie of maligned creatures in *Macbeth*: the blind worm who is libellously equipped with a sting, the owlet who donates a wing for the witches' cauldron, the hoarse raven who "croaks the fatal entrance of Duncan under our battlements", the owl whose shriek heralds Duncan's murder, the woolly bat, the "fenny snake" who has the misfortune to be filleted, the exsanguinated baboon, and, to exemplify another of Shakespeare's prejudices, the "blaspheming Jew" who graciously donates his liver for Macbeth's hallucinogenic scrying potion. Nothing, however, was better calculated to play upon the paranoia of an early Stuart audience than the rat itself: inconspicuous enough to insinuate itself into any crack in the wainscot, voracious enough to consume more than a beggar's portion of wheat or barley, fertile enough to produce an overwhelming progeny, and intelligent enough to avoid the more ham-fisted predatory ruses. It is fortunate for rat-kind that no one had realised that all of these supposed vices (all but the first of which have been regarded as human virtues) were mere inconveniences compared with the black rat's cardinal sin: it was a vector for the bubonic plague.

In fact, the politics of rat-hatred has at times become rather complex. For Catholics under Hanoverian rule, only brown rats were taboo. The "native" black rat (*Rattus rattus*) had supposedly been supplanted by the brown after the latter had come to England in 1688 aboard the ship that brought the Protestant William of Orange across the Channel on his mission to depose the Catholic James II. The story is doubtful even on the most superficial level (William was more likely to have been accompanied by black rats than by brown, since the latter dislike ships), but it was attractive enough for the Victorian naturalist Charles Waterton to employ a menagerie of imported cats to exterminate brown rats. He relished whirling them by their tails and bashing their brains out whilst intoning "Death to the Hanoverian", but when he was presented with a black rat in a cage, he commiserated with it, calling it a "poor injured Briton". Rarely has an animal conflict been so apt a metaphor for a human one.

Rats were rarely connected with taboos about cleanliness until the nineteenth century, when sewers were being introduced on a large scale, and the connection between rats and plague was not conclusively established until the twentieth century. Prior to 1800, rats were hated primarily because of their sexual and digestive appetites, not because they were seen as unhygienic. Rats were regarded as particularly lascivious creatures, and many of the accounts of witches' rat familiars emphasise this sexual dimension. In 1618, Joan Flower and her two daughters, Margaret and Philippa, were tried as witches for cursing the Earl of Rutland and his family. Their confessions mention that the devil came to them in the forms of a cat, a rat and a dog (named Rutterkin, Little Robin and Spirit). Philippa had suckled a white rat familiar at her breast for over three years, and Margaret "had two familiar spirits sucking on her, the one white, the other black spotted within the inward parts of her secrets". Ellen Shepheard, questioned in Huntingdonshire in 1646, was visited by four familiars in the shape of rats, who promised her that she would "have all happinesse", but in return they must "have blood from her, which she granted, and thereupon they sucked her upon and about her hippes." It is tempting to compare this link between the rat and female sexuality and spirituality to traditions in Indian mythology which hold that women possessed no sexual organs until the rat gnawed them into being. However, in contrast to the Christian tradition, this sexualisation of the rat is seen in entirely positive terms in the Hindu tradition, and to this day the temple dedicated to Karni Mater near the Indian city of Bikaner is crawling with very fecund sacred rats who are regarded as reincarnated human souls. Perhaps early-modern witches held rats in similar reverence. Perhaps too, they found that they were a cure for loneliness, as was certainly the case for an early twentieth century woman from Lelant, West Cornwall, an acquaintance of W.H. Hudson who entertained a wild rat in her kitchen. The woman, who was childless, allowed the rat to make its nest in her house, and even her pet cat befriended it, until the rat had the idea of pulling out the cat's fluffy facial hair to line the nest.

A vestige of much older traditions about the sexual potency of rats may have survived into the Victorian era in the folklore of the Toshers, or scrap metal scavengers of Bermondsey, in London. They repeated tales of the Queen Rat, a rat-like supernatural being who could transform into an alluring young woman and seduce an unsuspecting tosher. If the tosher failed to notice her rat-like characteristics (eyes which reflected light in the dark, claws on her toes) and made sufficiently passionate love to her, she would give him good luck, but if he detected her animal nature and shunned her, she would shape-shift back into a rat, and he would suddenly become alarmingly accident prone. In the case of Jerry Sweetly, who slapped the Queen Rat when she bit his neck at the height of her passion, the price was death and misfortune for his future sexual partners, although he always did well in business after their assignation. The Queen Rat also seemed to be capable of passing on some sort of genetic inheritance through the men she seduced, for amongst the children borne by their future sexual partners, there would always be a girl with mismatched eye colours, and very acute hearing. Once again, the rat is both admired and despised for being so like us: it exhibits an evident enjoyment of sex and a prodigious reproductive capacity. Since the sixteenth century, sensational literature has reproduced woodcuts – and later, photographs – of the Rat King, a veritable clump of rats (as many as thirty-two have been recorded) who have died after their tails have become entangled due to overcrowded conditions. There is something orgiastic about the Rat King; and suitably dried, it would make an ideal witch's fetish.

Nowhere is the ambivalent attitude of humans towards rats more starkly portrayed than in the iconography of St. Gertrude (631-659), who is regularly depicted with multitudes of rats in attendance. The orthodox Christian explanation is that the rats represent defiled sinners whom St. Gertrude is sanctifying, but as Sabine Baring-Gould argued so attractively in 1872, the rats are more likely to be fleeting souls, making St. Gertrude a successor to the Teutonic goddess Holda, who receives the souls of children. The Pied Piper of Hamelin, too, receives the souls of children after he is short-changed for his services in ridding the town of rats: a tradition which is not endemic to Germany, but was also applied to Francheville (now Newtown) on the Isle of Wight. The rat charmer himself, like the Fool of the Tarot, is also a liminal, underworld figure, who wears parti-coloured clothes and disappears into a cave, or across the water. Nor is he confined to a purely pre-modern existence, for in 1955 the journal *Folk-Lore* recorded the case of a travelling rat-charmer who would visit farms and mysteriously rid them of their rats by playing on a whistle and leaving written incantations in their holes. To have such an affinity with rats is to identify oneself with the underworld, or perhaps with that other celebrated, seductive piper, Death himself.

Rats are, indeed, often agents of retribution in western folklore. There is, for example, virtually a whole sub-genre of tales about cruel or irresponsible bishops who were eaten by rats. Bishop Hatto met this fate after stockpiling grain during a famine, and a sixteenth century woodcut shows the rats swimming out and boarding his boat like a horde of pirates in order to sink their teeth into his flesh. In 997, Bishop Wilderof of Strasbourg suppressed a convent and was duly consumed by rats, who were presumably incensed that they would no longer receive any charitable donations from the nuns' kitchen. Such traditions reach a deliciously macabre climax in Frederick William Orde Ward's narrative poem, 'A Legend of the Inquisition' (1890), in which a condemned man is punished by being tied face-to-face with his dead wife, and thrown into a dungeon. The "merciful" rats come in the darkness and devour his wife's corpse, relieving him of the burden of her decomposing flesh, but then they start on him, stripping away his eyelids, then his eyes and the skin of his face. As in Poe's 'The Pit and the Pendulum', a Protestant army arrives at the eleventh hour, and coming upon this scene of protracted torture, they capture the Inquisitors, lock *them* in the dungeon, and leave them to the rats.

The rat, like the jester, is despised and marginalized, but her trickery often points towards the truth, her jibes are often the work of justice, and her apparent cruelty is ultimately only the sly egalitarianism of Death, the leveller. Nowhere has the rat impinged more on the modern consciousness than in the trenches of the First World War. At times, the food chain was reduced to a single link: the rats ate the humans, and the humans ate the rats. "Do you remember the rats;" asks Siegfried Sassoon in his 1919 poem 'Aftermath', "and the stench/ Of corpses rotting in the front line trench?" Isaac Rosenberg's poem, 'Break of Day in the Trenches', is perhaps the most moving modern appropriation of the rat as a wise fool: "… a live thing leaps my hand/ A queer sardonic rat –/…Droll rat, they would shoot you if they knew/ Your cosmopolitan sympathies.

/ Now you have touched this English hand/ You will do the same to a German..." By crossing No-Man's Land, the rat may commune with the combatants of each side, and by implication, her stomach may be the scene for a strange meeting between the flesh of the British and the German dead. The parti-coloured piper comes to Briton and German alike, and the rat is merely a silent partner in the Dance of Death.

Like us, rats are creatures of habit. Indeed, there is something ritualistic about their behaviour. Portia and her progeny rapidly wore pathways in our front lawn, connecting the bird table to their various hiding-places, and then avoided departing from them. If a rat trail skirts around an object that is later removed, the rats will continue to take the diversion, as though the object were still there. Introduce a new object to the territory, and their suspicion is aroused. The sudden appearance of a new food source is likely to be ignored, to the frustration of those who leave out poison bait. Such furtiveness gives rats a reputation for intelligence: it is said that in order to steal an egg, rats will work in tandem, one lying on its back and holding the egg in its forelimbs, the other dragging its partner along by the tail. Part of us wants to attribute such sagacity to the rat, for despite our most malign efforts and our campaigns of extermination, statisticians insist that, especially in cities, it is rare for a human being to ever be more than a few feet away from the nearest rat. Perhaps the Hindu reverence for the rat has something to teach us — something we witches once knew, and have almost forgotten. As they burnt her alive, did Agnes Sampson go into a rat? We will know we approaching a sorcerous secret when this question no longer seems insulting. The witch, like Death, the jester and the rat, is always cleverer than she seems.

Chapter Nine

Cryptogams: The Spore-Bearing Plants

My over-active imagination was first influenced by the power of the non-flowering plants when I was nine years old. My father had picked some shaggy cap mushrooms, *Coprinus comatus*, growing under pines, and that evening, he seethed them in milk. I ate them with relish, then spat into my sleeve compulsively in fear of poison. I remember them well, still sizzling in their buttered bath, in a white dish, and the way their pink-white flesh slithered through my lips, a paroxysm of sense, the melting in the mouth of my first initiation.

Later that evening, the final episode of an adaptation of Robert Graves' *I, Claudius* was on television. I watched with delicious horror, my limited knowledge of mycological toxicology throwing my fancy into convulsions. Suetonius, Tacitus and Dio Cassius all agreed that Claudius was poisoned with a dish of mushrooms. Some sources add that the emperor's final meal was prepared by Locusta, at the command of his wife Agrippina. In all likelihood, Claudius thought that he was eating the prized esculent *Amanita caesarea*. A servant versed in elementary mycology would no doubt have found it easy to substitute one of these delectable orange-capped mushrooms for a specimen of the green-capped *Amanita phalloides*, aptly dubbed the Death Cap, the most poisonous mushroom in the world. Around ninety per cent of recorded deaths from mushroom poisoning are caused by this, and only a few grams are required for a fatal dose. It is hazardous even to breathe the spores, but the baleful effects of the poison do not exhibit themselves for around twelve hours after ingestion. By this time, there is normally irrevocable damage to the liver and other body tissues. After two or three days, the symptoms seem to subside, but this remission is the cruellest ruse of all, for afterwards comes delirium, coma, and slick and clammy death. Fortunately, my father knew his *Coprinus* from his

Amanita; indeed, he knew one *Coprinus* from another, for had he and my mother consumed the Shaggy Cap's near relative *Coprinus atramentarius* with their customary glass of wine, they would have been throwing up all night.

There can be few more fertile interchanges between science and lore than that which has revolved for centuries around cryptogams. The name itself is inspiring, for while on the surface it tells us, rightly enough, that the sexual lives of these plants are hidden and mysterious, the novice who begins to pay attention to them will quickly realise that so much more has been encrypted. Most witches, it is to be hoped, can identify a range of flowering plants, but spore-bearing plants are much more difficult to pin down. Perhaps we overestimate the difficulty sometimes, since it hardly matters if we cannot place a species of *Geranium*, but a misidentification of a species of fungus could be catastrophic. Ferns, with the exception of a few very common or remarkable species, are rarely differentiated in the folk mind at all, so much so that most of their 'common names' are merely translations of their generic and specific ones. Mosses, for most, are simply padding for plant pots, and the club mosses, despite their name, are only vaguely related. In order to become authoritative, one must be initiated into the mysteries, and this can only happen when one can speak the language, and distinguish a decurrent gill from one that is adnexed, or determine whether a rachis is branched or unbranched. And just when the arcane discipline seems to be mastered, more fundamental questions begin to vex the enquirer, such as whether fungi are really plants in the first place.

Nor is it surprising that Lewis Carroll placed his hookah-smoking caterpillar on top of a mushroom, for when it comes to exploring the lives and folklore of these plants, or researching the narcotic effects of a few of them, we really

Cryptogams: The Spore-Bearing Plants

are through the looking glass. The Siberian shamans known as the Koryak, for example, revere the Fly Agaric mushroom, *Amanita muscaria*, eating it to achieve transcendental states, and they tell the tale of Big Raven, who is charged with the Herculean task of rescuing a whale, stranded far from the sea, by carrying it in a big grass bag. He turns to the god of existence, Vahïnin, for aid, who tells him to go to the plains before the sea and look for "the spirits of Wãpaq", white soft stalks wearing spotted hats. Big Raven does as he is told, eats of the Wãpaq, and the gills turn and whirl like a kaleidoscope. He returns to the whale, finding that it has shrunk to a hundredth of its accustomed, blubber-threshing size. He dances for joy, flips up the grass bag with his little finger, and capers away with the whale like an archetypal eco-warrior, returning it to the deep. Amongst its other hallucinogenic and aphrodisiac effects, the alkaloid muscaridine does indeed cause partakers to perceive surrounding objects as either very large or very small, but any reader determined to test this should be warned that Fly Agarics also contain muscarine, a poison which causes acute gastro-intestinal distress. This, as the Koryac discovered, may be evaporated by baking or drying the mushrooms, and the hallucinogenic effects of the muscaridine can be accentuated by drinking the urine of someone who has partaken of the Fly Agaric.

Ergot, *Claviceps purpurea*, which grows on the seed heads of rye-grass, is another fungus containing psychedelic alkaloids: lysergic acid derivatives which cause the eater's vision to be suffused with brilliance, and which give men incorrigible erections. Unfortunately, they also cause fever, delusions, convulsions, swollen blisters, and atrophy of the extremities leading to gangrene and death. During the Middle Ages, outbreaks of ergotism were commonly known as St. Antony's Fire, after the wealthy Frenchman

Gaston promised his fortune to the cult of St. Antony if the saint would miraculously cure him and his son of the disease. It is probably significant that medieval portrayals of the temptation of St. Antony, with their plagues of vicious-looking demons, so often appear to be depictions of hallucinations. It has also been suggested that the Eleusian mysteries were probably caused by ergot poisoning, and it is also possible that outbreaks of witchcraft persecution, such as the Salem witch trials in Massachusetts in the early 1690s were also responses to delusions brought on by eating flour contaminated with ergot.

Other mushrooms have gained an occult importance not through the efficacy of their active ingredients, but because of their appearance or life history. The stinkhorn mushroom, *Phallus impudicus*, has always been valued in sympathetic magic. Gerard, it seems, had a fit of doubt as to the propriety of the creator, in whom he appears to have believed, for he printed his diagram of this fungus upside down in an attempt to disguise the obvious resemblance, but gave the game away when he named it: "Pricke mushroom, *Fungus Virilis, Penis effigie*". The undeveloped fungus is a round white ball, which reminds me of one of the devil's testicles, dropped when he was in a hurry, or perhaps cast aside during one of his ritual folkloric geldings. Dodoens (1563) thought that these rounded earth-heavers were the eggs of spirits or devils ("Manium sive Daemonum ova"), and a tradition amongst German hunters, who called the stinkhorn "Hirschbrunst", held that it grew where stags had rutted. Observation of this fungus over the period of a few days only serves to heighten its mystique. First it thrusts forth out of the ball, the shaft lengthens, and the sticky head aspires to sky. It grows foetid with the sweat of questing, quivers with the pulse of earth. If you listen, you can almost hear it groaning with sperm. At last, plied

Cryptogams: The Spore-Bearing Plants

by flies, it is primed for its own sickly orgasm; the glans all green and engorged, as though a breath of wind could make it blow.

Folklore surrounds other mushrooms too: the Jew's Ear Fungus, *Hirneola auricularia-Judae*, which, according to an anti-Semitic tradition, first grew on elder trees after Judas Iscariot hung from one, and is an everlasting commemoration of his suicide; and the fairy-ring champignon *Marasmius oreades*, whose spreading circular mycorrhiza have so long marked points of intersection with the otherworld. Some fungi, such as the Dryad's Saddle, *Polyporus squamosus*, have evocative names suggestive of forgotten lore. Others have real life histories which seem stranger than folklore itself, such as *Cordyceps militaris*. Airborn spores of this insignificant fungus land at random on a champing caterpillar upon a leaf, and germinate. Thereafter, the fungus parasitizes the larva as it pupates underground, its guts and wings and compound eyes becoming a tangle of fungal hyphae, until at last the *Cordyceps* bursts out of the withered coffin of a chrysalis, and marks the caterpillar's grave for long enough to spread the spores once more.

Reproduction by means of spores has itself become the stuff of legend. It has long been held that at certain appointed times, the "seed" or spores of ferns can give a person the power of invisibility. It is normally maintained that the spores must not be shaken from the frond, but persuaded to fall by means of a spell or "receipt". Shakespeare alludes to this folk belief in *1 King Henry IV*, Act 2, Scene 1, in which Gadshill insists that "we have the receipt of fern-seed, - we walk invisible." His companion, the Chamberlain, appears to be something of a sceptic, for he replies "Nay, by my faith, I think you are more beholding to the night than to fern-seed for your walking invisible." It seems likely that the belief was related to homoeopathic magic: the fact that fern spores are miniscule led to the assumption that they could confer invisibility. The theme is taken up in a little more detail by Richard Bovet's remarkable *Pandæmonium, or, The Devil's Cloyster, Being a further Blow to modern Sadduceism, proving the Existence of Witches and Spirits* (1684). Bovet, a Puritan reacting to the scepticism of the rising Enlightenment, argued for the existence of various supernatural agencies, insisted that the spells of witches were potent, and then went on to argue that the Roman Catholic Church was practising a form of witchcraft.

Much discourse [he added] hath been about gathering of Fern-seed (which is looked upon as a Magical Herb) on the night of Midsummer Eve, and I remember I was told of one that went to gather it, and the Spirits whiskt by his Ears like Bullets, and sometimes struck his Hat, and other parts of his body: in fine, though he apprehended that he had gotten a quantity of it, and secured it in Papers, and a Box besides, when he came home, he found all empty. But most probable this appointing of times, and hours, is of the Devils [sic] own Institution, as well as the Fast, that having once ensnared people to an Obedience to his Rules, he may with more facility oblige them to a stricter Vassallage.

It appears that Bovet eventually fell prey to the notorious Judge Jeffreys, and thus may have ended his days wishing that times were more enlightened than he had hitherto been willing to concede.

More obscure ferns than the ubiquitous bracken have been attributed with magical powers. When gathered by moonlight, Moonwort, *Botrychium lunaria*, is said to be capable of opening locks and loosening nails on hinges, and the alchemists believed it had the power to turn mercury into silver. Culpepper recorded that the plant was colloquially known as "Unshoo the horse", and insisted that Moonwort was responsible for an incident "On the White Down in Devonshire, near Tiverton, [in which] there was found thirty horse-shoes pulled off from the feet of the Earl of Essex his Horses…" *Osmunda regalis*, the royal or flowering fern is known in Cumberland as the Marsh Onion, because of the

Cryptogams: The Spore-Bearing Plants

whitish mass which grows within its rootstock. In county Galway, this "onion" is called the "heart of Osmund", which, when sliced, pounded and left to macerate, is said to be efficacious in cases of rheumatism. The Adder's Tongue, *Ophioglossum vulgatum*, was a popular remedy for snakebite; a rather far-fetched application of the doctrine of signatures, given that the fern looks nothing like its namesake. Lowlier cryptogams even than these have been exploited in societies where anything of the remotest utility was appreciated. *Sphagnum* moss is more absorbent than cotton wool, and the wounded at the battles of Clonterf and Flodden were not misguided when they stuffed their wounds with green bog moss and soft grass. Surgeons on the western front used it too. The Dutch Rush, *Equisetum hyemale*, a horsetail, contains so much silica that it was imported to Britain from Holland as a scourer. The spores of club mosses (*Lycopodium spp.*) were used, under the name of Vegetable Brimstone, as a waterproof coating for pills, and since they are flammable, were invaluable for pyrotechnics, stage lighting, and for the special effects employed by conjuring magicians and charlatans alike.

There is, as any true witch will tell you, much to be said for the attitude of Tolkein's Gollum, whose eyes were always cast down on the ground. The cryptogams were the first plants to colonise dry land. Once, there were club mosses which towered over dinosaurs, but now, the spore bearing plants are those which are most likely to be ignored. To know them is indeed to be initiated into the secrets of a living code, with permutations as infinite as spores. If we fail to notice them, it is our loss. They will still be here when we are gone, and some of them will be the prime agents of our dissolution.

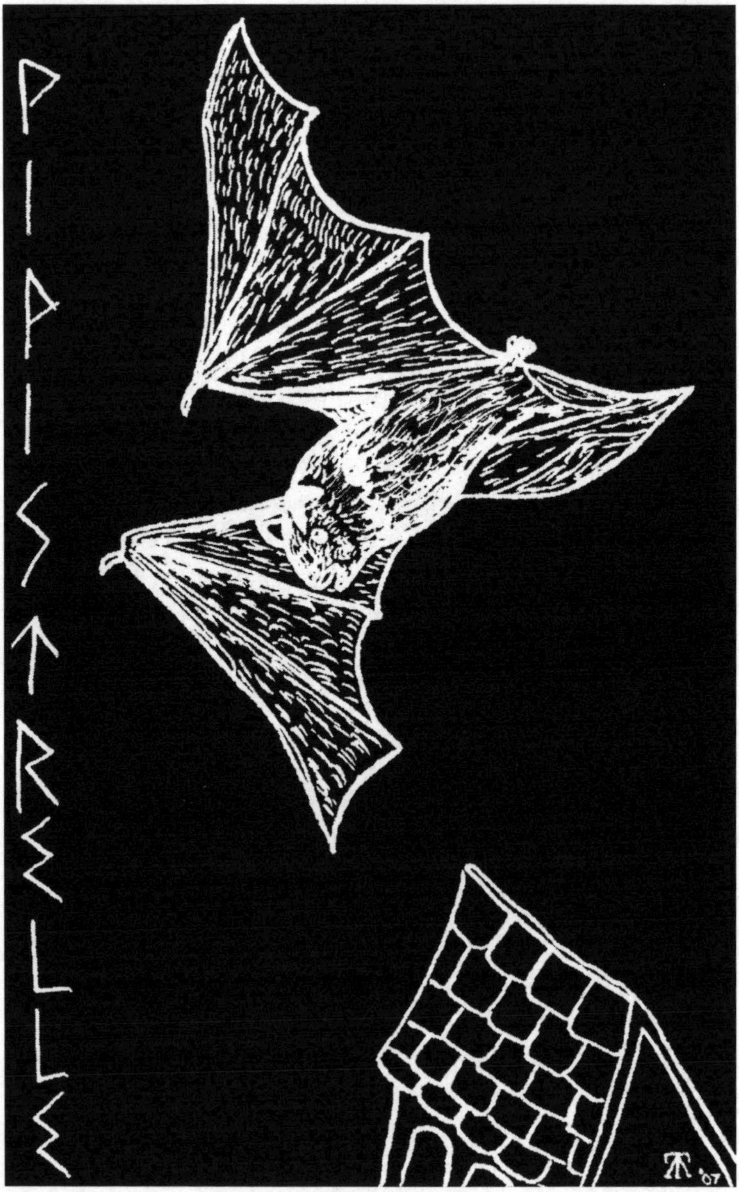
PIPISTRELLE

Chapter Ten
Through the Lychgate

Hans Holbein's engravings of *The Dance of Death* (1538) have always struck me as a sort of macabre Tarot. From one vignette to another, the semi-decomposed personification of Death comes to all conditions of men and women: the little child snatched remorselessly from beside the hearth; the quack physician abducted with his flask of urine; the nun swept away as she kneels at her devotions whilst her boyfriend strums a lute; the miser purloined from his counting-house; the king devoured at his table; the pope deprived of his tiara as a king kneels to kiss his feet. Death leads a blind old man into the churchyard, directing him straight towards his yawning grave. His skull wreathed with foliage, Death capers off with a hunch-backed old woman whilst another skeleton pounds on a xylophone. Towards the end of the sequence, the skeletons gather at the cemetery to celebrate in a throng, blowing on trumpets and beating on tympani with drumsticks made of long-bones. Finger-bones, ribs and skull fragments lie scattered on the ground, just as they do in the churchyard in my village, which was recently dug up for a drain. (It would, of course, be remarkable indeed to find a churchyard burgeoning with all of the fauna and flora described in this essay. The description which follows is an amalgam of my observations in a range of churchyards throughout Britain. The alkaline soils of my own local churchyard are not, for example, conducive to the growth of foxgloves, although other species, such as the yew, are ubiquitous). Behind them is a lychgate – literally, the corpse-gate, where the body lies in its coffin awaiting burial – the entrance to the churchyard. To pass through it is to pass under the shadow of Death; taken seriously on Samhain night, it is a sabbat-journey into the land of shadows and shades.

The full moon is obscured by the great yew to your left. Raise your lantern to it. Coolness seems to emanate from it as its dark fingers reach towards you. Nothing grows beneath it but its toxic companions, ivy and dog's mercury, which are scrawled across the red and powdered earth; grass withers beneath it, for all parts of the yew are poisonous, apart from the sugary red fruits that hide the seeds. The great bole's girth grows branches, each of them tree-trunk thick, all bristling with half-started shoots. Sit beneath the yew, and the needle-scattered roots envelop you. Great tufts of red twigs, peppered with fallen fruits, nut hard, and browned needles are piled like ants' nests. The green curtain of the foliage looks black by night, hanging almost to the ground. Folklore insists that the skulls of the dead are grasped underground by the roots of the yew, and the eye-sockets are occupied once more with living tissue. In his poem, 'Transformations' Thomas Hardy recognised the great pagan truth that lies behind such lore:

> *Portion of this yew*
> *Is a man my grandsire knew,*
> *Bosomed here at its foot:*
> *This branch may be his wife,*
> *A ruddy human life*
> *Now turned to a green shoot.*

Nevertheless, the nineteenth century *Dream Book* of Zadkiel says that if you dream of sitting beneath a yew, you have foreseen your own death. In the lantern light, the trunk seems to be splashed with specks of blood, turned ruddy brown. Fallen bark and needles ply the soil: dried warrior blood, woad and ochre, draining through the ground. Dream that you stand before a yew, says Zadkiel, and you shall live.

Come out from beneath the yew, and walk along the path that leads through the gravestones beside the church. A kestrel, roosting on a ledge half-way up the wall, twitters at you uncomfortably, but does not fly. A bat dodges past you, inches from your head, and moments later returns, as if tracing some arcane moebius strip through the air. Perhaps it is a Pipistrelle which has flown down from its daytime roost in the bell-tower. At any rate, you are lucky to see it, for the Pipistrelles are flying with less enthusiasm now that the autumn nights have lengthened, although their hibernation is less profound than species such as the Barbastelle. Daubenton's bat, which also frequents this churchyard, attracted by the stream beneath the willows beyond, has been hibernating since the end of September. The ancients were long confused by the nature of bats, being unable to decide whether they were beasts who flew like birds, or birds who wore fur and suckled their young. Aesop regarded the night-flying of the bat as a punishment for its duplicity in the war between the birds and the beasts, when it kept switching sides, and was ultimately shunned by both tribes and relegated to the darkness. In another fable by Aesop, a bat is twice attacked by weasels. The first weasel informs the bat that he eats only birds, whereupon the bat tells him he is a mouse, and is released. The second weasel specialises in mice, and is duly informed that his captive is a bird. Across the globe, the Cherokee tell the tale of a great ball game between the beasts and the birds. Rejected as team-members by the beasts because of their diminutive size, two mice climbed a tree and asked the eagle whether they could join the birds' team. The birds used a drum-skin to fashion wings for one, transforming it into a bat, whilst its companion was turned into a flying squirrel, and the bat's skill in aerobatics helped him to score the winning goal. For this reason, invocations to the bat and the flying squirrel are made by Cherokee lacrosse players in the ritual dance which precedes the game.Back in Europe in the early seventeenth century, the playwright Ben Jonson theorised in *Catiline* that "A serpent, ere he comes to be a dragon,/ Does eat a bat". Other folk tales about bats are darker in tone. The Mordvines of Russia make the bat an ally of Satan in his attempt to make a living human from the sand and mud of seventy-seven different lands. Unable to breathe life into the body he had created, Satan sent the bat to steal the towel of the Almighty, with which he rubbed the homunculus, bringing it to life. For its role in this caper, the bat was deprived of the feathers on its wings, and given a leathery tail and feet like Satan's; whether these were punishments or badges of honour is a moot point.

Indeed, Western traditions have consistently associated bats with the supernatural and the diabolical. A number of features of the bat's biology may explain this. Their nocturnal habits and uncanny ability to navigate in darkness have long been a source of wonder. Their rather humanoid looking faces, with elaborate facial appendages or ears equipped with a spearhead-shaped tragus (both of which seem to assist them in echo-location), combined with their paired breast-nipples, may make them seem like parodies of humanity. They may be demons, or they may, as in the Odyssey, be the shades of the dead, fluttering and gibbering in the night. In Sicily, they are specifically the souls of those who have met a violent death, whereas in Ovid's *Metamorphoses*, they are the descendants of the daughters of Minyas, Alcithoe and

Through the Lychgate

Leuconoe, who were turned into bats because Bacchus was enraged by their refusal to attend his orgies. Their tapestries transformed into ivy, and "they were lifted/ On no great mass of plumage, only on wings/ So frail you could see through them". Because bats are watchful by night (their eyes contain rod cells in profusion, but no cone cells, so that they cannot see colours), they have often fallen victim to crude sympathetic magic, finding themselves nailed alive to doors or window-frames to ward off evil, or hung in sheepfolds, as recommended by Pliny, to keep away wolves and other marauders. Pliny also attested that a woman could be made more pliable to seduction if a clot of bat's blood were placed under her pillow, a spell which was presumably ineffective if she was in the habit of plumping her pillow before sleeping on it. Albertus Magnus was fond of smearing his face with bats' blood in order to assist him with nocturnal divinations, whilst Gesner warded off demons with the mere image of a bat, engraved – unfortunately - on rhinoceros horn. A Tyrolean gypsy who wishes to be invisible may carry the left eye of a bat in his pocket. It is to be hoped that the modern witch would have greater sympathy with Lady Jacaume than with any of the former - burned for witchcraft in Bayonne in 1332 on the grounds that neighbours had observed a throng of bats frequenting her house and walled garden – or with a Chinese tradition that a person who kills a bat will go blind. The gloriously erotic kitsch of Luis Ricardo Falero's nineteenth century paintings of voluptuous witches in flight by moonlight, in the company of beautiful silhouetted bats may also deserve to be back in vogue.

Of still greater folkloric significance is the bat's habit of sleeping head downwards by day, almost completely encapsulated (especially in the case of Horseshoe bats) in their leathern wings, like corpses in suspended coffins. A beautiful Latin passage by the ornithologist Aldrovandus

(1681) describes the river Nyctipotus, which flows past the Isle of Sleep. This is inhabited only by bats who roost in giant mandrakes and poppies the size of trees; both plants have long histories as narcotics and anaesthetics. The deathlike sleep of the bat, which is still more profound when the animal's metabolism shuts down during hibernation, may also have fostered its association with European vampires. Although bats had long been used as symbols for the demonic in mediaeval art, culminating in their association with cannibalistic witchcraft in Goya's painting *Conjoro* (1798), their specific relation to vampires grew after the Conquistadors encountered true blood-sucking vampire bats in South America. It seems an uncanny coincidence, therefore, that recent medical scholarship has come to suggest that our western vampire legends were inspired by the observation of human victims of rabies, a horrendous disease of the central nervous system which is still almost always fatal if not treated before the symptoms arise. In the journal *Neurology* in 1998, Dr Juan Gomez-Alonso listed the symptoms of rabies in humans: hypersexual behaviour, insomnia, hypersensitivity to strong stimuli including aromatic smells such as garlic, aggressiveness and tendency to bite other people, facial spasms causing baring of the teeth, and frothing at the mouth caused by an inability to swallow fluids - characteristics which are in common with the Eastern European vampire tradition. Death by shock and asphyxiation, which is common in rabies patients, inhibits the clotting of the blood, neatly accounting for the long-dead bodies which spurted blood when a stake was driven through the heart. The Hungarian vampire frenzies against which the Empress Maria Theresa legislated so rationalistically in the eighteenth century may have been fuelled by the rabies epidemic which raged throughout the country between 1721 and 1728. Dogs and wolves were implicated as the main vectors, but the fact remains that all species of bat, not just vampires, can act as carriers, and because their teeth are tiny, their bites are often undetected. Rabies can also be spread to humans in aerosol form if they enter bat roosts. Such considerations may seem rather recondite on a cold night in October, but you are in the right place to be meditating upon them: to this day, rabies continues to cause 30,000 deaths a year worldwide, and whilst Britain is almost completely free of the disease, the most recent fatality here occurred in Scotland in 2002, when a conservationist was bitten on the finger by a bat. He would doubtless be the first to urge us not to visit our revenge for this accident of nature upon the bats themselves, who suffer as badly from the disease as its human victims.

The creeping cold arouses you from your bat-induced reverie. There are rustlings in the long grass as you wend your way between the older, lichened tombs. It is unlikely to be a hedgehog, for these have mostly found their way beneath wood-piles, ready for their winter hibernation – a good reason for shifting the logs before lighting the bonfire on the 5th of November. Perhaps it is the shrews, who are active throughout the winter, desperately sniffing out whatever insects, grubs or snails they can find in order to maintain their rapid metabolisms. Many of them die off as the weather grows colder; you may see one stagger out onto the path in front of you in the light cast by your lantern. It is surprising how few witches have claimed a shrew for a familiar: perhaps it is because shrews die too easily from sudden shocks. They certainly have one extraordinary characteristic to recommend them. Topsell, in his *Historie of Foure-Footed Beastes* (1607) claims that the shrew "is a ravening beast, feigning itself gentle and tame, but, being touched, it biteth deep, and poisoneth deadly". This observation was long thought to be an old wives' tale – but as is so often the case, the old wives were right all along, for experiments in the 1940s demonstrated that the tiniest quantity of extract from an American shrew's submaxillary gland was sufficient to kill a mouse. Shrew poison has similar effects to cobra venom, slowing the heart rate, lowering the blood-pressure and causing respiratory failure, but it also has painful localised effects similar to those of a viper bite: a burning sensation followed by shooting pains up the affected limb. In fact, the innocent little insectivore carries a poison every bit as baleful as the yew you passed on the way into his domain.

Alternatively, the rustlings may be caused by rodents: perhaps a long-tailed field mouse or two are cavorting amongst the nettles. These beady-eyed little creatures truly are harmless, but they have on occasion been confused with the Devil himself. In Devon in the 1860s, a great stir was caused when the "Devil's hoof-marks" were discovered in the snow, running along the ground for an estimated hundred miles, and even traversing roof-tops and haystacks. Great consternation was caused by the discovery that the tracks went right up to a stone wall, and then recommenced on the other side, as if the Devil had dematerialised and walked straight through it. This vexing mystery was not solved until 1964, when Mr Alfred Leutscher suggested that the hoof-marks were actually the impressions left by the long-tailed field mouse, as it leapt through the snow. When the mice leap, they "leave a U-shaped impression, 1½ by 1 in., at 8 in. intervals, precisely the dimensions recorded for the trails seen in south Devon in February, 1855." Wood mice, as they are also known, are also architects, constructing little cairns of stones above their burrows.

A mist is descending, and at times it seems to take corporeal forms as you pass the church and walk with your lantern swinging at your side, down into the darker parts of the churchyard which border the stream. Here,

Through the Lychgate

the grass has been allowed to grow much longer, and ivy festoons the crumbling monuments. The waist-high plant whose broad leaves have not yet withered in the frost is Belladonna, the Deadly Nightshade – whose leaves and berries are one of the principal ingredients of witches' flying ointments. A fifteenth century source attests that "The vulgar believe and the witches confess, that on certain days and nights they anoint a shaft and ride on it to the appointed place or anoint themselves under the arms and other hairy places and sometimes carry charms under the hair." When sparingly applied to the skin, the hallucinogenic alkaloids in Belladonna cause fibrillation – the sensation that one is flying – although ingestion is frequently fatal. An inquisitorial investigation into witchcraft in 1324 reports on one unfortunate adherent of the craft: "We rifled the lady's closet. There we found a pipe of ointment, wherewith she greased a staff, upon which she ambled and galloped through thick and through thin." Had she possessed a cauldron big enough to warm the water, she would no doubt have had a hot bath before applying the ointment, in order to open the pores of the skin, and aid absorption. In 1589, Porta, a friend of Galileo, went so far as to describe the effects of using Belladonna as an ointment, saying (to paraphrase loosely): "I am the grease-bird, eating grass; goose like I shall peck upon the ground. I shall become fish-fingered, fin-handed, fling out my arms and fly underwater; I shall float up and fly down, 'ere I die." It is oddly appropriate that the Deadly Nightshade is the food-plant for caterpillars of the Death's Head Hawkmoth.

Search further with your lantern, into the darker places. The plant with hairy, jagged leaves is Henbane, another member of the *Solanaceae*. Earlier in the year, its funnelled flower-heads looked like veined flesh, drooping with their own deep narcotic, their pistils like licking tongues; now its berries shrivel in the cold. In less enlightened times, Henbane was used as a pain killer, and was dubiously employed in fighting tooth decay. The normally quite astute naturalist John Ray described its use in 1660: "The seed of *Hyoscyamus* placed on a coal gives off a smoke with a very unpleasant smell: when passed through the mouth and nostrils by a tube it drives out small worms which sometimes grow in the nostrils or the teeth. They can be caught in a basin of water so that they can be seen better." The existence of these worms is attested by several other authorities, but dismissed by John Gerard, the herbalist, who described henbane-administering dentists as "mountibancke tooth-drawers". Like Belladonna, Henbane was added to flying ointments, and it was said that storms could be raised by throwing a portion of the plant into boiling water. Jon Hyslop and Paul Ratcliffe have more recently provided a recipe for raising spirits of the night by burning the herb with frankincense, fennel, cassia and coriander with black candles on a stump in a dim wood. "To be rid of them," they add, "burn Asafetida and Frankincense."

Other sabbat herbs may well grow in these far corners of the churchyard, which, it is satisfying to fancy, were once unhallowed ground. The hollow stems and umbel-shaped seed-heads of hemlock loom at head-height in the mist, although their characteristic purple spots and warning mousey smell may have departed by now. Socrates died drinking an infusion of this herb; a not suitable end, as Robert Graves once suggested, for a man who philosophised that trees and fields taught him nothing: men did. Germanic folklore maintains that toads gain their toxicity through sitting under hemlock plants and letting the dew drop onto their skin. The Greater Key of Solomon advocates that the blade of a sorcerer's black-handled ritual knife should be tempered in hemlock juice and the blood of a black cat.

Through the Lychgate

Another poisonous plant, the foetid Hellebore, may also grow in the churchyard, perhaps where it has been planted over a grave. Classical tradition relates that the shepherd Melampus first realised the medicinal qualities of Hellebores, curing the daughters of Proteus of their mental afflictions by giving them the milk of goats which had eaten the plant. Hellebores have also long been a folk remedy for worms, and a highly efficacious one at that, save for the fact that the poison often kills the patient as well. Dioscorides recommended describing a circle around the plant with one's sword before harvesting it. No bird must fly, and no sparrow make a sound, as one is plucking it, or the herb will be more poisonous than efficacious. Here, too, the dusty-leaved Wormwood – notorious as the active ingredient in absinthe - may grow. Cheiron, the healing centaur, first received Wormwood from the hand of Artemis, and dispensed the juice of it in crystal phials as a vermifuge and febrifuge. It is convenient that it grows here, since folklore has it that it is also an antidote to the insidious venom of the shrew. Another pharmaceutical wonder-plant, the foxglove, would have flowered here in the spring and summer. It is the source of the heart-stopping poison *digitalis*, which is used in measured doses to treat heart conditions to this day. It was used in the treatment of dropsy by a Shropshire wise-woman, Mrs Hutton, in the eighteenth century, but her secret was stolen by Dr William Withering, who published it as his own discovery in *An Account of the Foxglove and Some of its Medical Uses* (1785).

A shade-loving plant, Enchanter's Nightshade, grows under the trees beside the stream. It is named *Circea* after Odysseus's one-time lover and near-nemesis. Unlike the other plants you have encountered, this plant, with its little hairy seed-pods, has no psychoactive, medicinal or poisonous qualities whatsoever, and its romantic-sounding name is belied by its alias: Falsehood. Of course, in the skilful hands of Circe, it may have turned men into pigs, or perhaps she was able to raise monsters from the sea by pouring out a decoction of it, as in William Waterhouse's painting, *Circe invideosa*. Of greater use to normal mortals is the milky-white flowered milfoil or yarrow, which grows in great abundance throughout the churchyard. Pluck one of its highly divided leaves and look through it in order to see the fairies. Now, if you are single, search the headstones with your lantern. You are looking for the grave of a young maiden. Sibly says that you will need to return to this grave on the first hour of the morning, and pluck the yarrow that grows on it, saying, "Good morning, good morning, good yarrow/ And thrice a good morning to thee;/ Tell me before this time tomorrow,/ Who my true love is to be." Break the yarrow into three sprigs, and hide it in either your shoe or your glove, and return to bed without saying a word to anyone, and you are guaranteed to see your future lover in a dream. Given that it is Samhain, however, and you are here on a different quest, you had perhaps better save this frivolous piece of divination for another time.

There is one more plant, reviled by horse-owners but beloved of witches, which you must seek before your moonlit odyssey is quite complete. Its yellow flowers have now mostly gone to seed, and many of these have been carried off in the wind. Its leaves have been stripped to skeletons by the yellow and black caterpillar of the cinnabar moth, but it ought to still be quite serviceable for your purposes. Uproot the ragged Ragwort plant by the light of your lantern, for it is of little use to you in the ground: it is as a faerie-steed that the plant has earned its place in witch-lore. Both Burns (1785) and Henderson (1856) affirm that fairies and witches alike make use of it: "On auld broom-besoms, and ragweed naigs,/ They flew owre burns, hills and craigs." Grasp the stem firmly in both hands, and hold it between your legs. Somewhere in the distance, a fox rasps his backwards, steamy bark into the night. Across the stream, a roebuck has paused, and is watching you intently, quite unafraid. From the church tower, a barn owl screeches, her voice the trumpet-call of Death, and all at once, you are above the earth, ascending by horse and hattock through the sabbat-black sky, and the bat flies by your side, the lychgate far below.

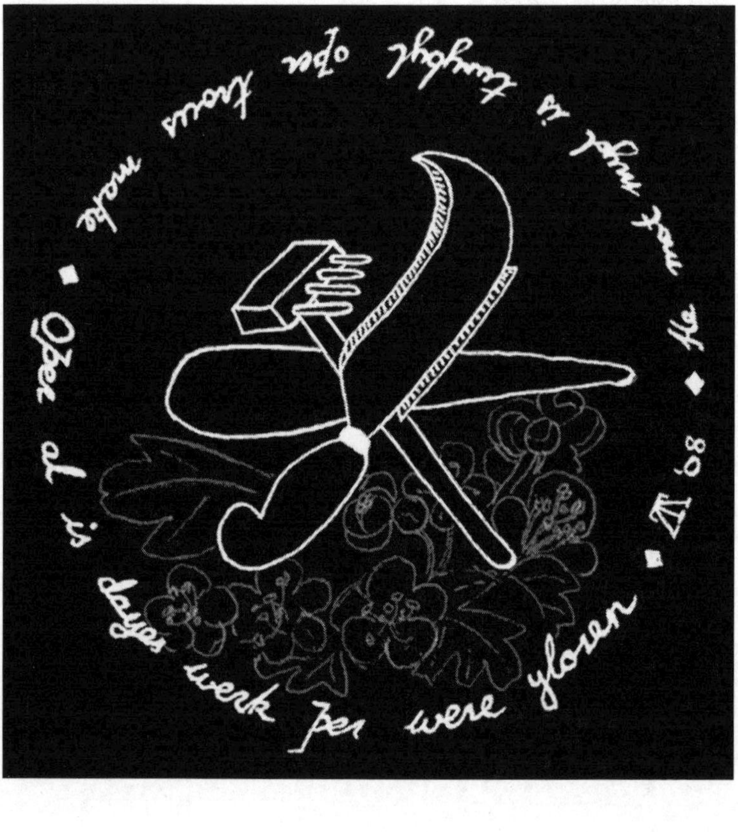
Oþer al is dayes werk þer were yloren

Chapter Eleven
The Witch by the Hedge

It is autumn, and the fecund hedge is heavy with fruits. I walk by its side, knee deep in hedgerow herbs for thirty yards, counting the species. I will not count the ivy, whose wormlike roots cling to the elder's bark, or the bramble, heavy with clots of bruise-coloured berries, but only the stouter shrubs and trees. The hawthorn predominates, its sex-scented flowers now replaced with ripening haws, the deep-green leaves beginning to blacken at the edges. The elder crowns nod heavily with berries. Here, an ash tree has grown to its full height, the branch tips aspiring upwards, the key-like seeds, still green, dangling and rustling in the wind. Beside it, a sycamore, cut to a height that will allow the passage of a leaping horse, spreads cool shadows. Crab apples are weighing their branches down, and the hazel yields cob nuts half-enclosed by withering bracts. Fine, divided leaves of maple flutter beside the stouter leaves of privet, already gnawed by portly caterpillars of hawk moths. Sloes, their flesh still green and bitter, punctuate the foliage of stunted blackthorns, and in the darker corners, holly berries are turning red. I count on my fingers, a hundred years for each tree, and with my last step, I meet with a spindle bedecked with pink baubles, each with four lobes packed with seeds. Applying Hooper's Rule, I can date this hedge with reasonable accuracy; it is one thousand, one hundred years old: a Saxon hedge, pre-dating the Norman

Conquest. It is an antiquity on a par with any of our great castles, a food source which has helped to maintain whole populations of humans, birds, insects and rodents for over a millennium, a refuge from the blade of the plough, and the subject of some of the richest folklore in the British Isles.

The hedge probably began life as a fence made of dead wood, the *haga*. Saxon farmers cut hawthorn boughs from woodland trees, binding them together with hazel withies. Here and there, where there were gaps in the fence, young hawthorn cuttings were trained across. The hedge itself stood on a bank, an uncultivated area of soil, which was quickly colonised by wildflowers and weeds. Birds perched on the fence, and passed the seeds of woodland trees in their droppings. These germinated, and instead of rooting them out, the farmers realised that they would only serve to make the fence more impenetrable. Gradually, as the dead wood of the fence rotted away, the gaps were filled with growing trees, and the hawthorn was planted deliberately, its thorns an effective deterrent to wandering cattle. When the Normans arrived, they brought rabbits with them, and tame falcons trained for hunting. The Norman lords appointed haywards to keep the hedges trimmed so that they would not impede the progress of the hunt. Gradually, it was realised that the hawthorn would survive being cut down through the stem nearly to the ground, so that the hedge could be layered, and the skill known as plashing, whereby a hedge was transformed into an impenetrable living barrier of thorn, leaf and wood, was developed into an art. By the thirteenth century, the art of the hedger was so sophisticated that a failure to hedge efficiently using living plants was considered a worthy subject for satire. In a lyric from the Harley manuscript, the Man in the Moon is lampooned as a foolish hedger who tries to patch the gaps in his hedge with cut thorn-boughs, hammered into position with stakes:

The Witch by the Hedge

Wher he were o þe feld pycchynde stake
(He's there in the field, struggling with stakes),
For hope of ys pornes to dutten is doren
(Hoping the thorns will close up the gaps)
He mot myd is twybyl oper trous make
(His twybill must chop and gather a bundle)
Oper al is dayes werk per were yloren
(Or else, alas, his day's work is lost).

The twybill was by now the traditional working tool of the hedger, edged on one side like an axe, and on the other like an adze, and the attempt to maintain a barrier with anything other than living materials was already recognised as a symbol of folly.

During the Black Death, the hedge grew wild, and the stronger plants grew into trees, warped by centuries-old plashings at the bases of their trunks. By the Tudor period, it had been tamed once again, and the herbs at its borders were prized as the ingredients for love-philtres. In the eighteenth century, the enclosure acts ensured that this venerable hedge was adjoined by younger upstarts, dividing the fields into orderly grids, and the poorer people, now without lands of their own, turned once again to the older hedgerows for their sustenance. By the nineteenth century, the hedgerow was the subject of bitter disputes between villagers and hedgers who relied upon it for survival, and gamekeepers who saw its denizens as vermin. In the early twentieth century, increased urbanisation had reduced the obvious utility of hedges, but they burgeoned as havens for wildlife. Older friends of mine still testify to the fact that before the 1950s, a walk beside a hedgerow was a very different experience, for the sound of the birdsong was almost deafening. Agitate a limb with a walking-stick, and clouds of insects would fill the air. By the late twentieth century, the art of the hedger was dead. Insecticides, fertilisers and herbicides turned the fields into deserts supporting one species, sustained not by organic processes but by large-scale hydroponics, and hedgerows themselves were ripped up to make way for combine-harvesters capable of servicing rape-fields measured not in acres, but in square miles. The folklore of the hedgerow lapsed into obscurity, so much so that many of those who today describe themselves as Hedge Witches would be hard-pressed to identify the species in my 1,100 year-old hedge, let alone venture an opinion on their magical uses.

Yet the archetypal association of hedges with witches remains. The hawthorn itself is the hag-thorn, whose blossoms may not be brought indoors, for "Hawthorn blooms and elder flowers fill the house with evil power". In all probability, this saying stems from a Christian prohibition. Fresh hawthorn flowers have the pungent smell of sex, and their whiteness and association with summer make them goddess-flowers, so it is likely that they were revered as such. In any case, folk traditions are unanimous in proclaiming that it is folly to cut down a hawthorn tree. A farmer who felled a hawthorn in Worcestershire broke both an arm and a leg shortly thereafter, whereupon lightning also struck his farm. At Clehonger, a farmer wishing to clear a field for rye-growing, took an axe to a hawthorn, and blood spurted from the trunk as from a severed neck. At Berwick St. John, a felled thorn tree blighted the land with barrenness, so that no hen would lay, no cow would give milk, and even the fallow deer stopped bearing fawns. More prosaically, in County Meath, the felled tree took its revenge when the farmer lent against a thorn, drove it into his skin, and subsequently contracted septicaemia and died. All of these popular traditions suggest an awed reverence for the

The Witch by the Hedge

hawthorn, whether because of its direct association with pagan deities, or because its gnarled trunks and branches, heavily grooved bark and thorn-serried fortresses make it in ideal abode for fairies.

The blackthorn, too, inspires an almost religious awe, and a staff cut from blackthorn has a long tradition as a magician's tool. The most notorious example is the gnarled staff of Major Thomas Weir, a pillar of the chapel-attending community in seventeenth century Edinburgh, until the day he stood up during a service and announced that he had long been in an incestuous relationship with his sister Grizel, with whom he habitually raised the devil and spirits of the dead. Strangled and burned for these excesses, Weir's ghost is still said to haunt the West Bow of Edinburgh, and is recognizable by his blackthorn staff. Another tool for maleficient magic is provided by the blackthorn in its thorns, which grow to sufficient lengths that they were once substituted for old gramophone needles, and remain the ideal biodegradable tool for transfixing wax poppets. The elder, although thornless, and useless for staff-making because of its pith filled stems, is another hedgerow tree with which one tampers at one's peril. The most celebrated of the elder witches is associated in folklore with the Rollright Stones in Oxfordshire, where the tree transformed itself into a woman in order to turn Viking marauders into stone, thereby creating the stone circle and outliers. The combination of the milk-white flowers, heady perfume, dark rich fruits and poisonous foliage make the elder a potent hedgerow plant, both in folklore and in practical magic.

Another hedgerow tree of particular significance to witches is the spindle. The pendulous, three-lobed, pink berries are poisonous, but twigs from the tree were, as the name suggests, used as spindles. There is no shortage of legends which maintain that an old spindle planted in the ground will presently grow leaves and become a tree once more: a very old folkloric motif, and one which suggests that the tree's magical powers of regeneration were the subject of veneration.

The climbing plants of the hedgerow are also magically significant. By an immemorial tradition, the final sheaf of the harvest has been tied with ivy, decorated with ribbons, and venerated as the Ivy Girl, a symbol of the coming of winter, and perhaps of the reign of dark goddesses. The bulbous root of the white bryony, another hedgerow plant with poisonous red berries, has long been used to make mandrake dolls when the real plant was not available, and like true mandrake, the root may be carved and re-planted in order to make it appear more realistically humanoid. Sir Hans Sloane (1660-1753) was the first to record the practice of sowing corn into the head of the mannikin and allowing it to germinate, thus imitating hair. In the Cambridgeshire fenlands, bryony mandrakes were collected on "Venus Nights", and displayed on shelves in the local inns, prizes of tobacco, beer and pickled onions being awarded by the landladies to the most anthropomorphic roots. The roots which failed to win these competitions were not wasted; they were chopped up and variously used as cure-alls and lucky charms kept in moneyboxes for the increase of riches, and in pigsties for the health of the piglets.

Any witch who has sought to cut a suitably impressive staff will have noticed, as Gerard did in 1656, that "The Woodbinde [honeysuckle] groweth in woods and hedges, and upon shrubs and bushes, oftentimes winding it selfe so straight and hard about, that it leaveth his print upon those things so wrapped." This effect is particularly pleasing when the honeysuckle chooses a sturdy hazel stem as its support, and a walking stick cut from such a stem is said to enable the owner to court a lover. Other, more diminutive plants associated with hedgerows have also been used in love magic.

The Witch by the Hedge

Elizabethan love philtres made use of the beguiling blue flowers and dove-foot herbage of the meadow cranesbill, which Gerard also recommended (when mixed in a potion with nine red slugs ground to powder and taken in claret before sleep) for the miraculous healing of "ruptures and burstings". In both cases, it seems likely that homeopathic magic was involved. The name "cranesbill" is derived from the beak-shaped stylar column, which persists as the plant goes to seed. As this apparatus dries up, the column comes under increasing tension, until suddenly it ruptures and the seeds burst forth. The seed is often shot for a distance of several yards, and the similarity between this and human sexual ejaculation may perhaps account for the plant's efficacy in love philtres.

Nor are taboos against cutting and uprooting confined to the giants of the hedgerow. Another relative of the cranesbill, Herb Robert, with its blood-pink flower and ruddy shoots, shares with the robin redbreast a long-standing folkloric association with that mischievous and sometimes vengeful sprite, Robin Goodfellow. Both the bird and the plant have been revered as sacred, and folk belief dictated that the killer of a Robin would never be able to have a cow milked without the milk turning to blood. To uproot a Herb-Robert may bring a similar inconvenience, or even occasion a death in the family.

Of all the hedgerow herbs, however, surely none has a more distinguished magical pedigree than St. John's Wort. Long used in rituals at the midsummer solstice, when it blooms, the plant partly owes its solar association to the bright yellow colour of its flowers, but perhaps this also refers to the fact that the herb causes photosensitivity when taken internally. At times, the leaves have a strong smell, described by some as "goat-like", and by others as "foxy". The plant has long been burned in the midsummer fires, perhaps originally, as Richard Mabey suggests, as a form of sympathetic magic intended to mimic and strengthen the power of the sun. The smoke from the burning herb would waft over the fields, ensuring a generous helping of sunlight, and protecting the crops. The ancient Greeks placed a plant called *Hypericum* above their religious statues to ward off evil spirits, and while it is not known whether this really was the plant which in modern times has inherited that generic name, it is certainly true that Christianity appropriated the plant for its own purposes, as a charm against demons. Originally sacred to the pagan sun-god Baldr, the Christians dedicated it to John the Baptist, claiming that the bloody colour obtainable from its leaves was intended as a reminder of his martyrdom. The Revd. Hilderic Friend reports that "About Hanover... I have often observed devout Roman Catholics going on the morning of St. John's Day to neighbouring sandhills, gathering on the roots of herbs a certain insect looking like drops of blood, and thought by them to be created on purpose to keep alive the remembrance of the foul murder of St. John the Baptist..." The insect in question was *Coccus polonica*, a sap-sucking bug. In a thirteenth century life of St. Hugh of Lincoln, a woman tormented by a "licentious demon" in the form of a man was instructed by another male spirit to take a sprig of St. John's Wort and hide it in her bosom. The demon-lover forsook her house whenever she kept it in place because, he maintained, it was "disgusting and stinking". The plant was, according to the same author, efficacious against poisons, including snakebite. Sir Walter Scott also alludes to the disdain with which demon-lovers regarded the plant, since one says "If you would be true love of mine/ Throw away John's Wort and Verbein." Oddly, the plant was good not only for banishing spirits, but also for raising them. The enlightened Reginald Scot, who incurred the wrath of James I by writing to quell anti-witchcraft hysteria, nevertheless affirmed in his *Discoverie of Witches* (1584) that it was possible to "raise the ghost of a hanged man with the aid of a hazel wand tipped with an owl's head and a bundle of St. John's Wort". Moreover, the resin glands in the leaves of perforate St. John's Wort, *Hypericum perforatum*, which look like tiny pin-holes, were reckoned by Paracelsus, champion of the Doctrine of Signatures, to be an effective treatment of "inward or outward holes or cuts in the skin".

For the witch of pre-modern times, the hedgerow served both as a pharmacy and as a larder, and indeed, no modern witch can advance very far in the craft without at least a gastronomic intimacy with its hips and haws, its sloes and bullaces and crabs. More importantly still, it has always been a magical and poetic inspiration. Whether viewed in spring, when the hawthorn tips punctuate the winter browns with vivid green, at the height of summer, when the foliage is milk-splashed with elderflowers, in autumn, when every bough is burdened with ripening fruits, both healthful and baneful, or even in winter, when the hedgerow is a gaunt skeleton of plashed boughs, dormant, leafless branches and forbidding, criss-crossed thorns, the living hedgerow is the place where nature and nurture are in equilibrium. In a modern age in which people span the globe in search of the mystical, the witch affirms that the otherworld is never further away than the nearest hedge.

Chapter Twelve

The Witch by Moor and Wood and Shore

The "secret, black and midnight hags" are waiting. He alights from his horse, his heel squelching into boggy ground. Behind him, a mosaic of moss and peaty pools stretches away to the horizon, buffeted by wind. There is not a tree in sight; the acid soil and exposure forbid the growth of anything above knee-height. Beside the pool at his feet, the moss draws water, a thirsty sponge plastered over the stone, inches thick, the air above it slick with moisture. Further out into the water, flowers hang above the surface like heads of nodding puppets, the stems blushing as if freshly bruised. Beneath the water, the plant bears little bladders, like shed reptiles' scales adhering to the leaves. Crustaceans swim between the submerged stems, and the bladders gape like mouths, toothed with bristles. One touch of a branched antenna, and the valve trap springs and expands. Sucked inside, the crustacean struggles in vain as the sealed door slams, its prison walls exuding the juice of death. It may share its death-cell with an assortment of other partially digested insects and crustaceans, some of them still alive and threshing their appendages ever more slowly. The man knows nothing of these struggles between microscopic titans; he turns up the hill towards drier ground, where the first clumps of heather struggle to retain a foothold. His eyes are set on a triple cairn at the top of the hill, so he does not notice the plant underfoot, with its pale, curling leaves, sticky with their own exudations. Midges convulse in their death throes, their wings hopelessly glued to the surface of the leaves. There are other diminutive plants here too, with spatulate leaves bristling with appendages, all oozing a substance as sticky and seductive as toffee. A fly struggles on one of them, adhering haphazardly by one of its bulging compound eyes, doomed to buzz itself into its own minor oblivion. As it does so, the other tentacles on the leaf bend inwards to further ensnare the victim. The man pays them no heed, for he is heading up to the higher, drier heath, his mind reeling with the import of his meeting with the minions of Hecate. A wildcat yowls and bares its teeth at him, arching its back and twitching its grey bushy tail, before disappearing amongst the ling; no domestic cat – perhaps it is Graymalkin. He is Macbeth, King of Scotland, bent on his own struggle for survival, anticipating his assignation with three witches, who have already divined that they will meet him on this "blasted heath".

Had Macbeth not been so oblivious to these struggles on a smaller scale, he might have knelt, and learnt much from the wortlore of bogland plants. The spasmodic death throes of their insect victims might have led him more quickly to his nihilistic conclusion that life "is a tale told by an idiot, full of sound and fury, signifying nothing." The crustacean-devouring water plant was Bladderwort (*Utricularia*), and its terrestrial cousin with the scroll-like leaves was Butterwort (*Pinguicula*), so named because the digestive juices exuded by the leaves are a sort of herbal rennet. Indeed, the leaves may be added to cream in order to form butter, provided, of course, one picks the dying flies off them first. Beside this was the Sundew (*Drosera*), perhaps the most easily recognisable of the bogland carnivorous plants. Moorland folklore insists that the Sundew and Butterwort, together with the liliaceous, yellow flowered Bog Asphodel, are injurious to sheep and cattle, causing weakness in the bones. Although the latter is indeed poisonous to cattle, it is probably the moorland environment itself which causes the problem, since the soil, and everything that grows upon it, is calcium deficient. Paradoxically, it is also said on Colonsay that cows that have eaten Butterwort are safe from supernatural maladies and elvish arrows, and they have at times been used in conjunction with whin and juniper as a charm against maleficient witchcraft. On the

Isle of Man, Sundew is traditionally used as a love-charm by hiding the sticky rosettes in the clothing of one's intended lover, but the token might just as easily be used as a signal for a clandestine assignation. Another plant of the upland bogs, the Bog Myrtle is used as an insect-repellant, emetic and vermifuge, and in the 1860s it will figure as the main ingredient of a regenerative beer made by the landlady of the 'Black Horse' in Ampleforth, Yorkshire. The glands in its leaves secrete a wax which can be made into fragrant candles.

Macbeth will not pause on his way up the hill to chew on the stalk of the Heath Rush, for he is reliably informed that it causes hare-lips. Nor will he stoop to rip up the "tormenting root" of Tormentil, which jilted lovers burn at midnight on Friday to compel their lovers to return. He is soon knee-deep in heather, whose pink or purple flowers are said to be stained with Pictish blood shed in battle. It has long been used for tanning leather, it makes a refreshing dry ale, and its bell-shaped flowers are tempting to bees. Robert Graves makes an obscure and tantalising reference to an Irish tale of the goddess Garbh Ogh, collected by Dean Swift at Lough Crew. She haunted the heather moors, riding in a cart drawn by elks, accompanied by ten giant hounds, all with birds' names, and she subsisted on venison milk and eagles' breasts. Perhaps she was a winter goddess, for with the flowering of the heather, she built herself a triple cairn of stones and settled amongst the blooms to die, like a spent queen bee. Other parts of the moor may be covered with Bilberries, also known as Blueberries or Whortleberries, a delicacy picked in Ireland in anticipation of the feast of Lughnasadh.

The calcium deficiency in these acid soils limits the range of fauna Macbeth is likely to encounter. A stag may cross his path, the whites of his eyes visible as he hurls himself away from the likely hunter. A hen harrier may wheel overhead. There are other moorland birds too: the "treacherous" lapwing, as Chaucer called her, roused from her nest into flop-winged flight. She lets out a succession of pies and weeps the further she flies, the wan sky catching her silhouette. Now she wings a lap around the lone man, leaving her little ones behind and tempting him to follow her. Should he tread amongst them, they will scatter, spindle-shanked and peeping, with eggshells on their heads. In the distance, there may be the cackle of a grouse, prey to the hen harrier. At another time, Macbeth might have come upon the "lek", a communal display ground used by the polygamous male grouse to attract mates. For now, the grouse pecks at the heather, scuds over sodden sphagnum bogs, bubbling and crooning to himself, and eluding the shadow of man. Since the reign of the gun-hung gamekeeper has not yet begun, he must also elude the tooth and claw of the native wildcat if he is to dance in his lek next year.

When Macbeth reaches the cairn on the flattened summit, the witches will ply him with a hallucinogenic brew. The ingredients sound disgusting, but most of them are code-words for herbs gathered somewhere in the lowlands. Shakespearean tragic heroes are fond of such places in a crisis: King Lear and his Fool came to such a place when he was insane, and learned wisdom. On his way back down the hill, a less preoccupied man might stop at a solitary rowan tree by a stone wall – the only standing tree for miles. He has need of it, for its white flowers and red berries make it a goddess tree, a tree of inspiration. He might need to pick his way through the gorse, for here it has not been piled and burnt, and were he of more tender disposition, he might repeat the old adage, "Kissing's out of fashion when the gorse is out of bloom." Little does he know that the witches themselves will retire to this thorny bower if ever

The Witch by Moor & Wood & Shore

they are pursued. But his thoughts are on matters of state: trivial, irrelevant questions to bring to this ageless place. Of course, in the end, the witches tell Macbeth nothing that the bladderwort in the bog, the wildcat in his path, the harrier in the welkin, or the bleak and pitiless moor itself could not have told him: the truth about himself.

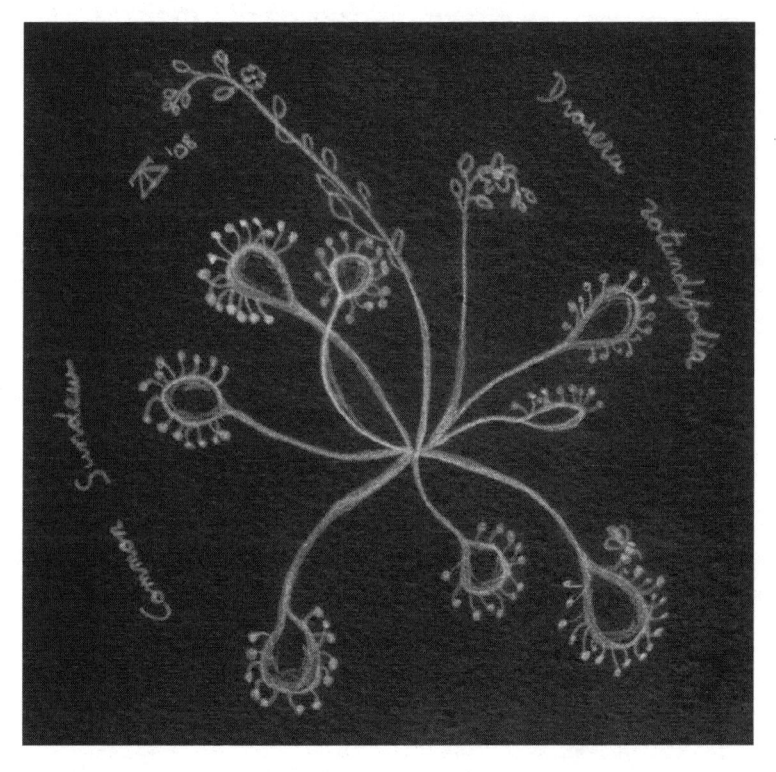

Of course, she is quite as beautiful as all of the other young Russian girls throughout history who have one day become wives to a Tsar: a simple, uncomplicated beauty which is scorned in her own house, but would be sufficient to light up the throne room in her future palace. But today, her brow is knitted in furrows and her body trembles as she runs. In her hand she clutches a little wooden doll, her magical saviour in times of crises, and her knuckles whiten for fear of losing it. In the distance, dimly visible between the moonlit boles of the birches, there glows a great arc of paired lights: a dull, greenish glow that sets her teeth on edge. Everything within her is telling her to seek the safety of darkness in the woods rather than hurry towards the ring of light, for she knows why the lights glow from paired orbs: they are human skulls, glowing in the sockets with a magical luminescence. Beyond the skulls, which are mounted on stakes around the perimeter of a fence knitted from human bones, there stands a wretched little hut – or rather, it doesn't stand exactly – it prances and scratches about in the dust, for it is mounted on a pair of grotesquely oversized hen's legs. A thin plume of smoke rises from the chimney of this hovel, and momentarily obscures the moon, for its occupant is at home. She is the Baba Yaga, a hideous hag who always puts her guests to the test, and eats them if she finds them wanting. No doubt she is also the lingering folk memory of a dark goddess, for when she is not flaying the skin from warriors' backs, she teaches her initiates the hard way, and they return to their own land filled with arcane wisdom. The young girl catches at the stitch in her side with her spare hand, and looks ahead in fear. She is Wassilissa the Beautiful, and whether she likes it or not, she is the Baba Yaga's next initiate into the mysteries of the forest – or, if she is unworthy, into the mysteries of the cauldron, as viewed from the *inside*.

When Wassilissa overcomes her fear and presents herself to the Baba Yaga, she is taken into the squalid hut and imprisoned there. On successive days, she is given a series of increasingly absurd and impossible tasks which need not concern us here, and whilst her magically animated wooden doll is wiping away Wassilissa's tears and solving all her problems, the Baba Yaga has locked the door behind her, climbed into her giant iron mortar, and is now flying out across the woods, rowing along through the air with her pestle, and sweeping away her trail with her kitchen broom. Some say she is off to fight magical battles in the chthonic underworld, but more likely she is off to seek her own wisdom from the woodlands that surround her home – or, given her novel mode of transvection, those farther afield.

Any normal mortal who explores a wood is likely to begin by searching for helleborines, twayblades or wood anemones in the spring and summer, or fungi in the autumn. However, for the Baba Yaga, like many other denizens of the forest, the odyssey starts not on the woodland floor, but in the treetops. Many of the birch trees in her own woodland carry "witches' brooms" – bunched and twiggy growths which hang from the branches. To the uninitiated, these look like clumps of mistletoe; in fact, they are galls caused by a fungus which persists from year to year, sometimes producing brooms a metre in diameter, and comprising three or four hundred twigs. A single birch tree may carry nearly a hundred such excrescences at the end of its comparatively short life span of a century. Amongst the plethora of galls which afflict the neighbouring, longer-lived oak trees, one of the commonest is the "oak apple": a rose-pink or yellow spongy ball of abnormal plant tissue which is the tree's defensive response to the insertion of parthenogenetic eggs into the developing bud by a wingless female cynipid wasp. Every oak apple is pleurilocular, containing around thirty chambers, each a cradle for a developing grub which gorges its bloated body on juices from the tree. In late summer, the imagoes gouge their way out, leaving the oak apples riddled with tiny holes. In Britain after the Restoration of Charles II, these curious plant-tumours were worn by Royalists on May 29th, Oak Apple Day, to commemorate his birthday and return from exile. In school, children who failed to wear the regulation oak-sprig were whipped with nettles. The oak was the ideal tree to symbolise the Royalist cause, given the popular rumour that the king hid himself from his Puritan pursuers inside a hollow oak tree at Boscopel. Although the fashionably sceptical Professor Ronald Hutton has persistently denied that the celebrations might pre-date the Civil War, many have concluded that Oak Apple Day is the remnant of a pagan fertility rite. Certainly, it has gained its own neo-Pagan associations in recent centuries. When Roger Deakin attended Oak Apple Day in the Royal Forest of Grovely in Wiltshire, he found a whole range of contradictions in the involvement of conservative country people in obviously pagan rituals, apparently supported by the church, and despite the Royalist history of the rites, deeply influenced by socialist responses to the Enclosure Acts. Oak Apple Day was an "annual reassertion of rights to collect wood" on common land. In the midst of this controversy, however, no one appears to have asked the obvious question, which is why oak apples specifically should be worn. It seems a strange – or, for those with republican sympathies, oddly appropriate – symbol of monarchy: a sham fruit, a spongy cancer writhing inside with parasitic grubs. As a symbol of fertility, however, it is potent: it reminds me of nothing so much as the ontological eccentricities of the sixteenth century miller Menocchio, resurrected for posterity by that admirable historian Carlo Ginzburg, who maintained that the origin of the universe lay in putrefaction: the world was a piece of cheese from which worms spontaneously arose. In any case, it is doubtful whether the Royalists realised that the wasps responsible for this ambiguous symbol have a curious and cryptic double life-cycle. In July, the winged imagoes mate, and the females penetrate the soil, for the next generation will be infants suckling on subsided sap, parasites not of growing buds, but of hidden roots in the humus. A descent into the underworld indeed.

In late July, the oak leaves are heavily mined by tiny caterpillars which live beneath the epidermis, most of them larvae of micro-moths. The Baba Yaga's flight through the canopy is the more pleasurable because of the Purple Emperor butterflies, largest of the *Lepidoptera* in northern climes. The male will choose the tallest oak for his throne, and will only be tempted to the forest floor by things white and glittering, or by rotting carcasses which he can probe with his hungry tongue. Perhaps the Baba Yaga will follow him: he is unlikely to find the carcase of a badger, for they like to intern their dead within their own setts, until their skulls, forever interlocked with their jawbones, are carelessly unearthed when the dwellings require extension. It is too late, too, for the flowers of the early purple orchid, whose tubers were once the source of the invigorating, semen-thick, starchy drink known as salop, a favourite refreshment of Victorian labourers, and a renowned aphrodisiac. It was once said that there were enough purple orchids growing in Cobham Park to pleasure every seaman's wife in Rochester. Perhaps this was another form of sympathetic magic: the twin tubers of orchids look like bollocks. The Purple Emperor flits on, over those withered stems, and alights instead on the corpse of a roebuck, already rotting. Its juices are rank and leaching into the soil, attended by burying beetles and maggots; the eye sockets are sunken. As the butterfly's tongue begins to probe, the Baba Yaga surely pays her respects to this horned one of the woods. Modern humans think of deer as the enemies of the forest, for they chew the shoots of newly coppiced trees. Whilst this is certainly true, there ought to be room for gratitude: a deer-filled wood is a bluebell wood, for the deer clear enough foliage for these plants to gain their requisite sunlight.

A Witch's Natural History

More importantly, in the Middle Ages, when forests were royal preserves, the trees were maintained as cover for the deer; without the deer, the woods would have been felled for pasture, and there would have been nowhere for Robin Hood to hide.

At the edges of the clearings in our wood of oak and birch, the smaller trees flourish. A hazel bends over a stream, waiting to drop its wisdom-filled nuts into the water, where, perhaps, the salmon of knowledge may swallow them. The spindle tree grows here too, and when all is gaunt in winter, her rose-pink, poisonous berries will shrink to reveal orange seeds: joyful punctuations of the prevailing gloom. No doubt the Baba Yaga has cut the spindle to make wands, for its white and lightweight timber is admirably suited. Indeed, it is said that a despairing seamstress who thrusts her spindle (derived from this tree) into the ground, will soon be delighted to perceive it taking root, producing greenish-white flowers and fruit as red as roses. No wonder the archetypal witch is often depicted with distaff and spindle.

These woods are the haunt of mustelids: not just the badger, but also the stoat and weasel. In winter, the stoat becomes the ermine, whose snow-white coat is a long and undulating sentence ending in a black full-stop: the tip of the tail. These tail tips, sewn with alarming profusion into trimmings of royal gowns, are the black wisps in the fluffy whitenesses which adorn the necks of mediaeval kings and queens, but in its natural state, the stoat is a wily creature with whom any witch should identify. Gamekeepers hate them, and cleave their skulls whenever they can find them, for they are crafty of mind and supple of body, and can take down creatures many times their size. The weasel is even smaller: a beady-eyed, ripple-bodied killing machine with teeth like needles. The late twelfth century Breton poet, Marie de France, who was a champion of misunderstood lovers and werewolves alike, has been one of the few authors (even the enlightened Kenneth Grahame fails in this regard) to ascribe noble qualities to the weasel. In her extraordinary lay known as *Eliduc*, the hero's lover lies dead, and his longsuffering wife feels for him in his despondency. She sits weeping beside the bier of the woman who has been bedding her husband, when all at once, a weasel runs past, only to be struck dead by a stick-throwing servant standing nearby. Moments later, a second weasel, the first one's mate, comes and finds her dead. He runs outside and picks a flower with his teeth, and uses it to revive her. In what must qualify as one of the most selfless acts in all romantic literature, Eliduc's wife retrieves the flower, resurrects her husband's adulterous lover, and graciously retires to a convent, and the weasels, one hopes, live on to perpetuate their species.

The mixed woodlands of oak, birch and ash lie in the lowlands. The beechwoods of the chalky uplands are quite different, and the Baba Yaga would fly far to find them. Mature beeches allow little sunlight to filter down to the forest floor, and as a result, the vegetation is sparse. One flower, however, has found a niche, and its perspicacity must arouse the admiration of any witch. The bird's nest orchid contains no chlorophyll, and as a consequence, it is not green, but yellow and fleshy, with a purplish tinge. The flowers are not gaudy, but brown, designed to attract flies, and the plant does not photosynthesise, for it is saprophytic, deriving its nutrients not from the sun but from an underground fungus with which it shares a symbiotic relationship – and the fungus, in turn, is dependent on the humus provided by the rotting foliage of the beeches. Every year, the orchid flowers by the bole of the beech, unless perchance its underground rhizomes encounter a stone. Should they do so, the plant will flower underground. A model of perverse and persevering persistence, it is surprising that the bird's nest orchid does not play a bigger role in folklore; indeed, the only explanation for this is the fact that it is hardly ever noticed, for without green colouration, plants are nearly always presumed to be dead.

It would be impossible for the Baba Yaga to frequent these woodlands without encountering a fox, and it would be unlikely indeed that she should fail to identify with him. Since the Middle Ages, the French have understood the fox most intimately, immortalising him as Reynard, the trickster who always has the last laugh. Sometimes he disguises himself as a monk, tonsuring the unsuspecting wolf with a cauldron of boiling water. On other occasions, he shams his own death, enticing birds within reach of his snapping jaws. Chaucer lets him sink his teeth into the neck of the narcissistic cockerel Chantecler, and in the mediaeval French romances, he even creates a martyr, Coupée the chicken, whose earthly life was so cruelly cut short. He presides laughingly over the castration of his rival Tybert the cat by a fornicating priest, and personally engineers the trapping of Bruin the Bear inside a cleft oak. Ever victorious, Reynard is the archetypal guiser. If you don't believe it, seek him out yourself in a summer glade where the rabbits are chewing cowslips: he sidles along, respectfully distant, and all at once he is turning somersaults as though he has gone mad, biting the dirt and threshing at his own tail with his hindlegs. The rabbits are mesmerised by this vision of a predator turned insane; slowly they creep closer. Reynard's game is an eloquent essay in predatory hypnosis. One rabbit strays too near, and the muscles ripple on the fox's muzzle, the canines bared. The pupils in the yellow irises congeal into sharp lozenges of dark. Suddenly, the fox-fool is a lethal machine, and the rabbit curls, screaming in agony in the fox's jaws. The Baba Yaga is not dissimilar in her dealings with her own victims.

The Witch by Moor & Wood & Shore

When winter comes, the broadleaved woods are bare, and only hollies and the occasional yew can relieve the monotony. At this time, no doubt, the Baba Yaga steers for the coniferous woodlands, eschewing only those of larch, which alone among the cone-bearing trees are deciduous. She seeks a creature every witch should revere. Of course, if we have had any contact whatever with modern environmental movements, we in Britain are immediately sure what creature she is after. It must be the red squirrel – that totemic creature whose imprint ensures fundraising success for every wildlife charity. Ousted from the woodlands of the south of our islands by the American grey – so this myth insists – the red squirrel persists in the Scotch Pines of the Highlands, staunch to the end like some latter-day Dad's Army. We conveniently forget that it is we who introduced the grey squirrel, so that we can demonise it, and that it is we in our unprecedented population explosions of the twenty-first century who turn our woodlands into minute islands in the sea of homogeneity, dooming the less resilient species to extinction. But the Baba Yaga does not seek the red squirrel. She is after something far more elusive: a lissom-limbed creature whose every movement is sinuous, smearing pungent scents on the bark of the pine bough. His pelt is the warmest brown: dark chocolate laced with white, and had he not been persecuted to near extinction in our country, the grey squirrel would never have extended its range. Should the fresh meat run out, he is resilient enough to resort to caterpillars, or even bilberries. These days, it takes a witch to find him, led onward by the pricking of her thumbs, and even then she must crane her neck, or mount once more to the treetops in her mortar, for this creature scampers where most men scorn to look. Furtive, trembling with the pulse of a hungry metabolism, the pine marten claws the bough. Like the eyes of Wassilissa's doll, its pupils are aglow.

The path beneath my feet is an ancient wickerwork of the roots of elms, and the ivied trunks beside me are columns in a cathedral of green, for Dutch Elm Disease has never ravaged the trees on the Isles of Scilly. Chiff-chaffs and wrens, roof-boss creatures come to life, peer between the leaves with beady eyes, and beside the raised path the little fenland supports a hundred tiny chapels of hemlock water dropwort, twinkling woodbines, and green and fleshy liverworts on gleaming walls of soil. A choir of hoverflies is singing, a tracery of elm twigs arching above them. I am on my way through the shrine to nature known as Holy Vale, heading towards Porth Hellick, a bay gouged into the granite on the eastern side of the island of St. Mary's. As I emerge from the fenland, where herons and egrets curl their harpoon-headed necks like question-marks, the dromedary-shaped geological feature known as Camel Rock looms in front of me. Shallow sea-water laps over the bladder-wrack as I make my way past it, and out in the deeper water, I glimpse the arched Roman-nose of a grey seal, his nostrils flared to drink in the air. Suddenly, he submerges, and I time the interval before his re-emergence, not daring to hold my own breath. He has exhaled before diving, every pocket of air expelled from shrunken alveoli, his bloodstream constricted, for this reduces his buoyancy. His blood is almost black in colour, for it is packed with haemoglobin in order to carry additional reserves of oxygen during the dive. Three, four, five minutes, and his head is bobbing up ahead, like a stub-nosed buoy with whiskers. Gulls skim the sea's dark undulations. A cormorant dives, and turnstones cry. The sun turns the sea mercurial, and the shoreline is a mirror with a glazed meniscus. As the old seal breasts the surge, I almost hear the slop of mercury, and then the sun shifts, the sea a green glaze crusted with foam. The boulders beside the path are mounded with unsalvaged disjecta: a winkle, a pebble, a cormorant's skull.

Beyond Camel Rock, an ancient stairway has been cut into the stone. Ahead of me, the cliff forms a great overhang, known locally as Clapper Rock. One can imagine it rapping like a gargantuan castanet on a windy night, and in the past I have taken children here on bivouacs, and they have scared each other sleepless with tales of the ghosts of suicides. As

I mount the stairs, the light intensifies; the stones seem to be vibrating. Spectral figures climb the stairs ahead of me, shawled and murmuring, disappearing behind a curve in the rocky cleft. I know who they are. In 1750, Robert Heath wrote the first ever book about the Isles of Scilly, and in it he described a collective of Healing Aunts whose traditions had been handed down from time immemorial. "They are all good *Botanists*," he tells us, "and have added a great many Herbs to their *Catalogue*... Their *Systems* and *Hypotheses* are to help those in Distress for Pity's sake rather than for Profit." In 1750, the most senior amongst them was Sarah Jenkins, a wise-woman and midwife of considerable local standing. That she was also a witch seems very likely: in her youth she certainly knew of the fairies which inhabited the chambered cairn of Buzza Hill near Hugh Town, whose "nightly *Pranks*, *aerial* Gambols, and *Cockel-shell* Abodes are now quite unknown." Supposedly, they were *"charm'd"* or *"conjur'd* out of the islands" by cunning-men from Cornwall, but surely I have seen them myself, belted with leather of *Laminaria*, their menfolk in britches of kelp, their women skirted with *Porphyra*, with purses of bladder-wrack, stitched with strands of *Chorda*. I am sure that to this day they dance to tunes of fiddles fashioned out of the skulls of guillemots, and beat on urchin drums.

I think I know where the ghosts of the Healing Aunts are going. They are heading across the heath towards the beach of Pelistry, beyond which lies Toll's Island, a grassy clump of rock connected to the beach by a sand-bank at low tide. In the eighteenth century, Toll's Island would have hung under a pall of noisome smoke, for it was covered with kelp-pits tended by wizened old ladies puffing perversely on blackened clay pipes. The kelp was burned to a fine ash and then exported for use in glass-making, a meagre source of revenue for the poverty-stricken island folk. Beyond the kelp-pits stands Pellew's Redoubt, a relic of the Civil War, from which not even these islands, twenty-eight miles into the Atlantic, were entirely free. At the far end, the sea slops and gurgles against the rocks, and it is here, I am sure, that the Healing Aunts are heading. The rockpools here are a candy-shop of colours: *Coralina* plants, articulated like puppets and pink as musk, kelps, oar shaped, made of chocolate leather, and edible sea lettuces, pistachio green. I bend down and dip my hands in the water. There is the sideways scuttle of a retreating crab, a frightened goby's blinkless eye, the urchin's serried army bristling. There are limpets and pixie cups and slowly moving snails clearing trails in sand. Despite the turmoil and pounding of the sea, delicate anemones spread their tentacles, or lie above the waterline like globules of blind red jelly.

Here the Healing Aunts will find Dillisk, a membrane-thin ribbon of red seaweed known to the Scots as Dulse, *Rhodymenia palmata*. Shawled in ragged wool, Sarah Jenkins bends hunchbacked over the rocks, plucks with scrabbling fingers the limp Dillisk from the stone, or rolls up her grubby sleeve, and picks it where it swells in swirling ribbons underwater. It clings to her skin as though it has been smeared with bacon grease. Rich in iodine, Dillisk has long been an essential component of the diet of coastal peoples, and during the Irish potato blight, it doubtless saved lives. Hanging in the kitchen, it withers at the edges, grows a powdery crust of salt, and stiffens like red parchment, until wet weather leaves it hanging flaccid: it is, in fact, the world's first barometer. Combined with sea lettuce and mixed with oatmeal, it is fried to make nutritious cakes. The seaweed known as "Irish moss" grows here too, its fronds rainbowed with bioluminescence under water. Medicinally, it is an anticoagulant, and a treatment for bronchitis, bladder infections and kidney irritation; it is also an effective gelling agent. The seaweeds are used here for fertilisers too, and wrack-cutters were equipped with special scythes for the purpose of harvesting the larger plants. Other seaweeds had folkloric significance: Viking descendents on Iceland were afraid of a hideous child-eating troll-woman named Grýla, whose coat was made of seaweed, and whose fifteen tails were made of the knotted wrack, *Ascophyllum nodosum*. In addition to her child-devouring cat, she had a string of husbands, none of whom could bear her carnivorous habits for very long, until at last she found a sort of happiness with Leppalúði, who was able to quell his nausea for long enough to father a multitude of offspring upon her, all of whom preyed upon human children. Similarly, Norse burial grounds on the Orkneys were later identified as homes of the Trows, semi-aquatic monsters who preyed on human souls. According to Jo Ben, writing in the early seventeenth century, the Stronsay Trows "very often go with the women there", and they are clad in red seaweed, with horse-like bodies. A Trow's penis, too, "is like that of a horse", and the testicles are particularly large. At the opposite extreme of Britain, Scilly too is covered with cairns and tombs, and it seems reasonable to suppose that in former ages, these also had their fair complement of seaweed-clad monsters. On a windy night on Scilly, it is difficult to believe that they do not exist.

No doubt the Healing Aunts did not confine their ministry to St Mary's. There are five inhabited islands in Scilly today, but in their day, Samson too was inhabited by two wind-worn families, the Woodcocks and the Webbers, who eked out an existence by fishing and kelp-burning before they were evicted in the nineteenth century by the lord of Tresco, Augustus Smith, who built a deer-park on the island, only to find that the deer scorned the place and swam back to Tresco. It is certain that there were magical traditions – not all of them entirely benevolent – on the other islands too, for the well of St. Warna on St. Agnes was once filled with bent pins, each designed to cause a shipwreck, and St. Agnes herself is represented in paintings with a stang, luring tall ships onto the rocks. However, today I will follow the Healing Aunts back to Hugh Town, and take their spectral boat to Samson. On the way, a sandwich tern is above me, slouch-winged and still in the air as a strained lever. All about the boat now, they hover, their necks cocked like flintlocks, their stretched wings bracketing the wind, the watchspring wound, near to breaking. The flintlock springs, and one bird makes a soundless plunge, harpoon-billed and hollow boned. For a moment, it is a stab of white cleaving the water. A sand-eel writhes, and the tern bursts shimmer-feathered back into the air. Riding this swell in winter, I might meet the Immer Loon, or Great Northern Diver, a bird whose ancestors once swum with ichthyosaurs.

There is no jetty on Samson: the spectral boat beaches on the sand of Bar Point at low tide. The beach is a white hump, with a single line of weed. At the top, there is dune grass bleached by brine, and in the spring, pyramidal orchids bloom in profusion. On Dune Hill, the first of Samson's two granite humps, there is a string of cairns from the days when Scilly was known as Ennor. There is yellow furze, gnarled ling, and a petering path, lined with thrushes' anvils, each with its own snail-shell cairn. Always, there are the wind-flayed sternums of gulls, rock-pipits, and once fearless wrens, the bleached wings still attached. I will follow the Aunts down the hill, towards the spume-worn Neck, and enter this empty, roofless home to my right, stooping beneath the rafter that would have been. There is an uncanny, unfathomable silence. I can almost hear the wheeze of a Woodcock, his clay pipe clenched in stained incisors. The air here is thick, and it is hard to breathe, for there is an emptiness, like the orbs of a gull's skull. Up the slope towards South Hill, another house beckons me, armpit deep in foxgloves and red-campions, and fringed with nettles - nitrogen-loving plants which frequent the past abodes of human beings. The hard-hewn lintel is perched precarious as a bird, and inside, the low hearth is lichen-bearded. There is the same silence, the same thickness, the same constriction of the throat; I know I am breathing ghosts, not air. I half-hear the sigh of a Webber, worn from kelp-burning, aching to rest her legs beside the fire that would have been. And now I am back out into the vacancies of brown bracken, walking by bluebells, grown wild from some garden long-gone.

The silences of Samson, here at the Atlantic end of the British Isles, hold within them the profoundest lesson a witch can learn. We humans are transitory: we are walking ghosts. Our hearths encrust; our lintels fall. Our clay pipes lie crushed in the strand. Our remnants are chipped flints, stone bottle stoppers, plastic flotsam. Our broken boats encrust with goose-barnacles. The Healing Aunts knew this: they have brought me here so I may know it too. The wounds we inflict on nature are skin deep; it will master us in the end. If you don't believe me, take the tourist-boat to Samson – the modern Scillonians will gladly take your money. Sit up there on South Hill and listen. Hear their yawls and cries. Glance down at their mottled eggs on the peaty pathways. Samson does not belong to human beings. It is owned by gulls, and the ghosts of all that would have been.

Chapter Thirteen
Beyond the Crooked Stile

It is said that Mother Goose is derived from Frau Holt, or Herodias, the goddess of the witches of northern Europe, who flies at night astride a goose, naked and (even in my childhood imagination) voluptuous in spite of the cold. She flies at the head of the Furious Horde, the Wild Hunt, her raven hair streaming out behind her, her red slitted pupils glowing on Samhain night. To be sure, she flies above the Ridgeway, where the feet of the living and of the dead have passed for millennia; a spirit path if ever there was one. At Bishopstone in Wiltshire, it draws nigh the Icknield Way, the Iron Age road to Norfolk, and between the high road and the low road lie a series of colossal gouges in the chalk

A Witch's Natural History

which even the tourist guidebooks describe as "another world". Five miles to the east, the chalk escarpment is rippled by glaciation to form "the Devil's Step Ladder", and beyond it the Uffington White Horse, smattered in spring with an interpunction of twayblades and spotted orchids, seems set to leap across the downs. Beneath that is a hill with a flattened top, where St. George purportedly slew the dragon, its blood scouring the grass to the chalk beneath it. There are few landscapes which contain so awe-inspiring an arrangement of sacred objects. The best way for the witch to approach them is from the Ridgeway itself, down one of the many paths that branch from it, and to do so, one must invariably negotiate a stile. Perhaps one day you may meet me at one of them.

In times of old, you might have left a crooked sixpence there. Weyland the Smith, whose megalithic forge lies just off the Ridgeway on the route between Uffington and Bishopstone, would certainly have accepted it, provided you did not attempt to fob him off with a lesser coin of copper. The Neolithic long barrow, sentried by four gaunt, pitted sarsen stones, is surrounded by towering beech trees, whose nuts crack underfoot as one approaches, and barn owls screech in the darkness. Come here at the winter solstice, with the rising of the sun, and the shadows shift like ghosts around you. Legend insists that Weyland will shoe your horse; I have a suspicion that he prefers to beat swords and axe-heads upon his forge, for he is not so far removed from the Green Knight, the Holly King who reigns throughout the winter, armed to the teeth in readiness to meet his rival, the Oak, on the occasion of his beheading. His namesake, the Icelandic Völundr, once decapitated a king's sons by slamming the lid of a treasure chest down upon their necks; later he raped a princess who asked him to mend her ring. The stone at nearby Snivelling Corner was supposedly thrown by Weyland at an incompetent assistant. It is best not to bother him with trifles. But this does not stop wayfarers from leaving behind an assortment of charms, from elaborately woven corn dollies to the Rastafarian wicker man currently on display at the Uffington museum – a practice which dates back at least as far as 1939, when a "Witch's moon dial", made from human bone, was deposited there. Mary Chalmers, a woman skilled at curing cows and sheep, who lived at Little Moreton, east of Didcot, was the proud owner of a skull named "Wayland Smithy", which was sold in a curiosity shop after she died in 1810. Satanic rites at Weyland's Smithy have even been blamed for a robbery at the thirteenth century church at Compton Beauchamp in 1998, in the course of which the tabernacle was smashed, and the chalice and sacrament stolen – if the churchwarden is to be believed – for nefarious uses at the long barrow.

On a morning in early spring, the Smithy is a different place; cowslips sprout from the burial mound, and the beech buds burst with pale, translucent leaves. The resident toad, who lives beneath the beech tree to your right, emerges glass-eyed from his torpor. Everything is waking, except for Weyland himself, who sinks into the earth as the sap rises in the trees. From here, one may turn east, dodging the cagouled walkers, and return to the White Horse and the hill fort that rears above it, listening for the cronks of ravens on the way. Alternatively, one may descend towards the Vale, seeking Hardwell Camp, another fort which lies forgotten, brooding in a hazel coppice. Or one may turn up one's collar and head westwards down the Ridgeway, towards Russley Downs and Bishopstone. If you would come with me now, you will take this route.

No, do not look up yet to admire the scenery, and if you tarry until the autumn, do not be distracted by the berries of sloe, spindle, bryony and woody nightshade. Look down at the Ridgeway itself. You are walking on prehistory, for surely the Roman road must have been pre-dated in these parts by a pathway joining the White Horse to the Smithy. More than that; you are walking on the palaeontological past, for the chalk of the Ridgeway is composed of the microscopic remains of Palaeozoic sea creatures. The rounded, flattened stone which just crunched beneath your walking boots is an echinoid, a sea urchin, millions of years old, revered by the old witches and Doreen Valiente alike as "thunder stones" or "shepherds' crowns". More than a hundred miles from the coast, you are now beachcombing on the Ridgeway. Pick up the test, and your witch's intuition will feel the pulse of life still within it. On the underside is the beaked mouth, crusted with chalk. On the dorsal side there is a five-pointed star. Treasure it in your pocket, and use it for sortilege, along with the petrified bivalve and the knob of coral you found beside it. Keep searching, and you will discover that these are not uncommon; the challenge is to find a brachiopod, a little clam with a muppet-like mouth. The exultation of this discovery should carry you in a reverie all the way to Russley Downs.

As you draw near to your destination, a hare darts and jinks in front of you. It has shot from out of hiding in the undergrowth at the side of the Ridgeway, like a bolt from a crazed crossbow, fired by a drunkard through a maze of mirrors. It is not by accident that the verb "to jink", used to describe the hare's habit of rapidly changing direction in flight from a pursuer, has affinities with the word "jinx". The crooked path of the hare has helped to establish its reputation as a magical creature from time immemorial. The ancient dramatist Aeschylus records that Artemis, who had always opposed the expedition against Troy, was enraged when two eagles devoured a pregnant hare, which the diviner Calchas interpreted, to her further indignation, as an omen of the victory of Agamemnon and Menelaus. Boudica, the Briton warrior queen, driven into a fury by the rape of British women by Roman soldiers, released a hare in the course of a rite in honour of the war goddess Andraste, before a retaliatory raid in which captured Roman women were skewered on spears, their breasts severed and stuffed in their mouths. It is possible that the hare represented the Romans Boudica intended to hunt down, but it is equally likely that the release of the hare was the unleashing of a curse. Even the Christian tradition is unable to obscure the magical significance of hares. A late medieval saint's life which very likely reflects the influence of an earlier pagan tale, the *Historia Divae Monacellae*, records that a hare pursued by Brychwel Ysithrog, Prince of Powys, took refuge under the skirt of the kneeling Saint Melangell, and his dogs cringed in terror at the sight of her. At her trial in 1662, the Nairnshire witch Isobel Gowdie confessed that she had the power to change into a hare at will by reciting the charm: "I shall go into a hare/ With sorrow, and sighing, and mickle care,/ And I shall go in the Devil's name/ Till I come home again." Indeed, there are innumerable folk tales from across the country which attest to the ability of witches to transform themselves into hares, a fact which is taken as proven when a woman is found with an injury corresponding to that inflicted on a hare by its pursuers. John Monro, an eighteenth century doctor who ran the Bethlehem hospital for the mentally ill, better known as "Bedlam", recorded the case of a Mr. Walker, who had been in the company of the devil for seven years, and had seen a vision of "the fall of all mankind". Mr. Walker attributed his affliction to a hare he had killed some twenty-seven years earlier, "which he did not think to be a common hare but… something he knew not of what infinite power." It is not surprising, therefore, that you feel an affinity with this creature, as it scarpers bulge-eyed down the gorge to your right. It beckons you on its crooked way.

Here, therefore, you must depart from the Ridgeway, for your path lies through that gorge in the chalk. At present, there is only a metal gate, but you will feel that you have climbed a stile. Half way down, it is marked on either side by two thorn trees. The gouged hill rears on either side of you. Linnets twitter. Black-faced sheep stare at you. You feel as though you are on a processional way to the underworld; you left your sixpence in case you need to cross the Styx. It is fitting that it is littered with innumerable carcasses. They are partridges, their flayed sternums, wishbones and coracoids gleaming white, picked clean of red flesh. Their wings lie as though dropped by accident, like forgotten handkerchiefs. A mournful whistle overhead; a buzzard takes wing. Crows wheel and craw. You descend to the depths of the gorge, your progress halted by a stile beside a spring. The silence here is uncanny, and you acknowledge another ancient presence. Strip lynchets rear to your right, traversed by the trails of bullocks. Strange optical illusions cause the landscape to writhe as you walk through it. You may climb the stile and pass through a wooded tunnel, lined with hart's-tongue ferns, to the twittering world of Bishopstone and its duck-pond, or you may turn aside and walk back uphill another way, for the gorge down which you walked has been joined by another. Look up the second gorge. It is surmounted by a colossal field system. Scramble up the hill towards it; a stairway for giants. When you reach the top, sit and stare. The mundane world stretches out beneath you: Swindon with its monstrous, magic roundabouts barely besmirches the landscape. The Vale seems interminable, stretching into mist, and something within you has taken flight, with the buzzards and the crows. Above you and behind you: a stile, and the Ridgeway, awaiting your return.

Beyond the Crooked Stile

As I sit here beside you, I can still remember the voice of my father; he was younger than I am now, and I was only four. I was ready for sleep, and he was reading from Mother Goose:

> *There was a crooked man*
> *And he walked a crooked mile*
> *He found a crooked sixpence*
> *Upon a crooked stile…*

I knew then that this was not a nursery rhyme, but a canticle of the Craft uttered by Fraw Holt herself, and I have sought the crooked mile ever since. It is crooked because it is the way of the hare, of the shape-changed witch, and because it must negotiate a course between sacred objects. It is a mile in the more liberal sense of the world: negotiating it may take a minute, or it may take a lifetime. The sixpence is the price of my soul. The stile is a real one, leading down into the gorge above Bishopstone, but it is also a metaphorical one. It is a gateway to the otherworld, the world of the sabbat. Against it, the crooked man leans his staff; beneath it lies the pot of ointment which gives him, his crooked mouse – and their crooked cat – the gift of flight.

Epilogue
The Living Bones: A Meditation

When I was eleven years old, I collected my first skeleton. It was scattered across the tussocky foothills, and its component bones surely originated from more than one animal. Some of them were new enough that they required bleaching to remove the traces of desiccated muscle, mummified integument. Some were half buried in the soil, encrusted with the scats of rabbits and of wombats, their ivory surfaces worn to reveal the once-marrowed honeycombs of bone beneath. Some were still connected: whole sections of vertebral column held together by dry cartilage, arched by sunning brown-snakes who fled at my approach. At home, I perused the diagram in my much-worn copy of Edmund Sandars's *A Beast Book for the Pocket*, assembling an ungulate version of a Frankenstein's monster in bone, until at last the entire sheep skeleton lay, assembled but disarticulated on the parched and weedy lawn.

Nearly thirty years later, and thousands of miles to the north, the thrill of skeleton-seeking has not subsided. The skull of a roe deer adorns my altar – one of my most treasured possessions. I found its owner in his death throes on the side of the road, mortally wounded, and held his head in my lap as he died. Then I lifted his body over the grassy verge at the side of a wood and laid him down, invoking sexton beetles and bluebottles for his funeral. Six

Epilogue

months later, I remembered him, and there he lay, picked clean, and sublime as ever. Another spirit-house, the brain-heavy skull of a crow, gapes upon my mantelpiece; I found this on a gamekeeper's preserve, the lower jaw still intact. It is a litmus test for the sensibilities of visitors to my home: will they be delighted or appalled?

Skeletons have been revered for time out of mind. Badgers periodically unearth them from their own setts. Elephants fondle them, seemingly recognising their long-dead relatives. The sanctuary circle at Avebury began its life as a charnel house, where human bodies were stored in varying stages of decomposition. Only when the flesh and skin had gone would the dry bones be removed to long barrows such as that at West Kennett. Bones were stained with ochre by the very earliest of humans, and traditional witches are known to practise the ritual of the red bones to this day – an important aspect of which is the visualisation of one's own skeleton. Skulls are fetish objects for pre-industrialised cultures throughout the world. Death is traditionally personified as a skeleton, and his dance is not unlike a seduction, with a joyousness all of its own. We are prone to forget, however, that the skeleton is designed for life, and not for death: that without it, we would have no blood, or at least, not any that we would recognise, and that every vertebrate possesses one, whether of cartilage or bone.

Let us meditate for a while on the living bones of a bird. Perhaps it is one of the pair of ravens who perform aerial somersaults above a part of the Ridgeway where I walk most weekends. That great, black beak is bone underneath its sheath of bird-horn, and the jaw is cleverly articulated for maximum gape. The orbits which accommodate the eyes are enormous compared with our own, and sclerotic bones hide within the eyeball itself: delicately interleaved flakes of calcium carbonate which form a ring like the diaphragm inside a camera. Fill a raven's skull with water and measure its cranial capacity; in ratio to the bird's body-weight, it will rival our own – a comparatively reliable guide to intelligence. There are multiple vertebrae in the neck – unlike the meagre seven allocated to all mammals, sloths excepted – and they have different functions in different parts of the neck, allowing the raven to put its head underneath its wing, or transfix you with a stare delivered from behind. Each process of each vertebra is a housing for a muscular attachment, facilitating this extraordinary mobility.

The pectoral girdle of the raven is a complex arrangement of fused but flexible bones. The clavicle, or wishbone, triangulates with the coracoid like the girders of an iron bridge, forcing the wings clear of the body whilst the raven is in flight. An elongated scapula corresponds to our shoulder blade: another surface against which muscles adhere. The sternum joins the coracoid, protecting the internal organs, and providing a deep keel to accommodate prodigious flight muscles the colour of plum-flesh. The humerus is heavily pneumatised so as to reduce the density of the raven for flight, and it is strengthened like the wings of a modern aircraft with internal bony struts. The radius looks surprisingly like our own, but the ulna is thin and barely complete, serving as an anchor for the secondary feathers of the wing. The bones of a raven's hand are fused but flexible in order to absorb the force of air pressure against the primary feathers.

Below the pectoral girdle, the bones of the vertebral column and the ribs are deeply interlocked and often fused, forming a dense cage enclosing the lungs, which do not float free in the chest cavity, but are joined to the connective tissue inside. The kidneys are protected by a platelike pelvic girdle, reinforced to stand the repeated pressure of landings.

Epilogue

It terminates in the pygostyle, ignominiously designated the "parson's nose": the anchor for the feathers of the tail. The femur, or thigh bone, is very short and packed about with enormous muscles; the knee is normally hidden close beside the body of the bird, so that the part a casual observer might identify as the thigh is in fact the tibia, and the long scaly shank beneath the bird's ankle appears to be its shin. The toes and claws of the raven are adapted for perching, but also for grasping its prey, and when the raven dismembers a dead animal, the talon anchors the morsel so that it can be torn into convenient strips by the bill.

Imagine the raven freeze-framed, poised in the middle of one of its characteristic aerial manoeuvres. Its bones are the scaffolding of life: the keel encasing heart and lungs and liver, the limbs adapted for the twin stresses of flying and landing. The whole skeleton is an essay in complexity, beauty and adaptability. For the witch it is also an esoteric glyph of a hundred and more articulating parts: simultaneously a design for life and a sigil of death.

The winter is blisteringly cold, and on this chalky rooftop of southern England, the wind hurls the rain remorselessly into my face. The ravens are above me as I lean upon my walking-staff, their trademark cronks echoing out across the valley. Always, they are ragged silhouettes, riding the tempest at unnerving speeds, swooping over a farmhouse a mile away, and returning in a moment. I am insane with the wonder of it, laughing into the gale. I think of the child with the jigsawed skeleton on the sun-scorched lawn, and know that I will never grow too old for the part of me that rejoiced then and rejoices now: the kernel that is witch. Black without, bleached white within, the ravens sing their hoary love-song to the wind.

Bibliography and Further Reading

ABURROW, Yvonne, *Auguries and Omens: The Magical Lore of Birds*, Berkshire, 1994.
ADAMS, Lionel E., *The Collector's Manual of British Land and Freshwater Snails*, Leeds, 1896.
ALLEN, Glover Morrill, *Bats: Biology, Behaviour and Folklore*, New York, 1939.
ANDERSON, J.R.L. and GODWIN, Fay, *The Oldest Road: An Exploration of the Ridgeway*, London, 1975.
ANDREWS, Jonathan and SCULL, Andrew, *Customers and Patrons of the Mad-Trade: the Management of Lunacy in Eighteenth-Century London*, California, 2003.
ANONYMOUS, *The Harley Lyrics*, Electronic Text Centre, University of Virginia Library, http://etext.lib.virginia.edu.
APULEIUS, *The Golden Ass*, translated by Robert Graves, Harmondsworth, 1950.
ARISTOPHANES, *The Frogs and Other Plays*, translated by David Barrett., London, 1964.
ARMSTRONG, Edward A., *The Folklore of Birds*, London, 1958.
BAKER, Margaret, *Discovering the Folklore of Plants*, Princes Risborough, 1999.
BARBER, Richard, *Bestiary: Being an English Version of the Bodleian Library, Oxford M.S. Bodley 764*, Woodbridge, 1999.
BARING-GOULD, Sabine, *Curious Myths of the Middle Ages*, London, 1872.
BATE, Seldiy, 'Big Black Crows', *Pagan Roots: Esbat Music*, London, 1994 (audio cassette).
BEVAN-JONES, Robert, *The Ancient Yew*, Macclesfield, 2002.

Bibliography and Further Reading

BOWLEY, R.L., *The Fortunate Islands: A History of the Isles of Scilly*, Berkshire, 1968.
BRACKENBURY, John, *Insects and Flowers: a Biological Partnership*, London, 1995.
BRIGGS, Katharine, *A Dictionary of Fairies*, Harmondsworth, 1977.
BRISTOWE, W.S., *A Book of Spiders*, London, 1947.
BURT, Jonathan, *Rat*, London, 2006.
BURTON, Maurice, *Wild Animals of the British Isles*, London, 1968.
CAMBEFORT, Yves, 'Beetles as Religious Symbols', *Cultural Entomology Digest*, second issue, February 1994, http://www.insects.org/ced2/beetles_rel_sym.html
CHINERY, Michael, *Insects of Britain and Western Europe*, London, 1993.
CHUMBLEY, Andrew D., 'The Leaper Between: An Historical Study of the Toad-bone Amulet; its forms, functions and praxes in popular magic', *TC*, 2001.
CLARE, John, *Selected Poems and Prose*, (edited by Geoffrey Summerfield and Eric Robinson), Oxford, 1964.
CLARKE, Howard and BURDEN, Vera, *Discovering the Ridgeway*, Pembrokeshire, 2002.
COCKER, Mark and MABEY, Richard, *Birds Britannica*, London, 2005.
COOKE, M.C., *Our Reptiles: A Plan and Easy Account of the Lizards, Snakes, Newts, Toads and Frogs, and Tortoises Indigenous to Great Britain*, London, 1865.
COOKE, M.C., *The Woodlands*, London, 1879.
COOMBS, Franklin, *The Crows: A Study of the Corvids of Europe*, London, 1978.
COOPER, Jane and SMITH, Sharon, *The White Horse and the Village of Uffington*, Witney, 2004.
COPELAND, Marion, *Cockroach*, London, 2003.
CROSS, Tom P., and SLOVER, Clark Harris (Eds.), *Ancient*

Irish Tales, New York, 1936.

DAWKINS, Richard, *The Ancestor's Tale: A Pilgrimage to the Dawn of Life*, London, 2005.

DEAKIN, Roger, *Wildwood: A Journey Through Trees*, London, 2007.

DEGRAFF, Robert M., *The Book of the Toad*, Cambridge, 1991.

EDLIN, Herbert L., *The Tree Key*, London, 1978.

ELLIS, Arthur Erskine, *British Snails: the Non-Marine Gastropoda of Great Britain and Ireland*, Oxford, 1969.

FABRE, J. Henri, *The Life of the Spider*, (undated), translated by Alexander Teixeira de Mattos.

FABRE, J.H., *The Glow-Worm and Other Beetles*, London, 1919.

FINLAY, Winifred, *Tales of Sorcery and Witchcraft*, London, 1980.

GERARD, John, *Historie of Plants (1597)*, republished as *Gerard's Herbal*, Middlesex, 1998.

GINZBURG, Carlo, *The Cheese and the Worms: The Cosmos of a Sixteenth Century Miller*, London, 1980.

GOMEZ-ALONSO, Juan, 'Rabies: A possible explanation for the vampire legend', *Neurology*, September 1998, 51:856-859.

GORDON Lesley, *Green Magic: Flowers, Plants and Herbs in Lore and Legend*, Exeter, 1977.

GRAVES, Robert, *The Greek Myths*, London, 1960.

GRAVES, Robert, *The White Goddess: a Historical Grammar of Poetic Myth*, New York, 1948.

GREEN, Miranda, *Celtic Goddesses: Warriors, Virgins and Mothers*, British Museum Press, 1995.

GREENOAK, Francesca, *British Birds: their Folklore, Names and Literature*, London, 1997.

GRIEVE, Mrs. M., *A Modern Herbal*, Surrey, 1973.

GUEST, Lady Charlotte (Trans.), *The Mabinogion*, reprinted London, 2000.

HARDY, Thomas, *The New Wessex Selection of Thomas Hardy's Poetry*, selected by John and Eirian Wain, London, 1978.

Bibliography and Further Reading

HARDY, Thomas, *The Return of the Native (1878)*, London, 1999.

HARE, C.E., *Bird Lore*, London, 1952.

HART-DAVIS, Duff, *Fauna Britannica*, London, 2002.

HEATH, Robert, *A Natural and Historical Account of the Isles of Scilly*, London, 1850.

HICKIN, Norman E., *The Natural History of an English Forest*, London, 1971.

HOLDER, Heidi, *Crows: an Old Rhyme*, London, 1987.

HUDSON, W.H., 'A Boy's Animism', in *Far Away and Long Ago*, London, 1939.

HUDSON, W.H., *Nature in Downland*, London, 1923.

HUDSON, W.H., *The Book of a Naturalist*, London, 1919.

HUMPHRIES, Rolfe (Trans.), *Ovid: Metamorphoses*, Indiana, 1983.

HUSON, Paul, *Mastering Herbalism*, London, 1974.

HUTTON, Ronald, *The Stations of the Sun: a History of the Ritual Year in Britain*, Oxford, 1996.

HYSLOP, Jon and RATCLIFFE, Paul, *A Folk Herbal*, Oxford, 1989.

INGOLD, C.T., *The Nature of Toadstools*, The Institute of Biology's Studies in Biology, No. 113, London, 1979.

JACKSON, Nigel Aldcroft, *Call of the Horned Piper*, Chieveley, 1994.

JACKSON, Nigel, *Masks of Misrule*, Berkshire, 1996.

JACOB, Dorothy, *A Witch's Guide to Gardening*, London, 1964.

JEFFERIES, Richard, *At Home on the Earth: A New Selection of the Later Writings of Richard Jefferies*, (Jeremy Hooker, Ed.), Devon, 2001.

JORDAN, Michael, *Mushroom Magic*, London, 1989.

KEAR, Katherine, *Flower Wisdom*, London, 2000.

KLANICZAY, Gábor, 'The Decline of Witches and the Rise of Vampires', in *The Witchcraft Reader*, (Ed. Darren OLDRIDGE), London, 2002.

KRITSKY, Gene and CHERRY, Ron, *Insect Mythology*, Writer's Club Press, 2000.
LAWRENCE, D.H., *Selected Poems*, (Ed. Keith SAGAR), London, 1972.
LAYARD, John, *The Lady of the Hare*, London, 1944.
LELAND, Charles Godfrey, *Gypsy Sorcery and Fortune-Telling (1891)*, (reprinted at http://www.sacred-texts.com/pag/gsft).
LEWIS, Mary, 'Witchcraft and Wizardry in Wales', from *The Queer Side of Things (1923)*, (reprinted at http://gaslight.mtroyal.ab.ca/gaslight/wizwales.htm).
MABEY, Richard, *Beechcombings: The Narratives of Trees*, London, 2007.
MABEY, Richard, *Flora Britannica*, London, 1996.
MABEY, Richard, *Food For Free: A Guide to the Edible Plants of Britain*, Glasgow, 1972.
MALORY, Sir Thomas, *The Morte Arthur*, in Eugene VINAVER (Ed.), *Malory: Works*, Oxford, 1971.
MARIE de France, *The Lais*, translated by Glyn S. Burgess and Keith Busby, London, 1986.
MARZLUFF, John M. and ANGELL, Tony, *In the Company of Crows and Ravens*, Yale, 2005.
MATTHEWS, L. Harrison, *British Mammals*, London, 1952.
McGREGOR, Alasdair, 'The Pied Piper', *Folk-Lore*, Vol. LXIV, 1955.
MORRIS, F.O., *A History of British Birds*, London, 1870.
MÜLLER-EBELING, Claudia, RÄTSCH, Christian and STORL, Wolf-Dieter, *Witchcraft Medicine: Healing Arts, Shamanic Practices, and Forbidden Plants*, Vermont, 2003.
NEAL, Ernest, *The Badger*, London, 1958.
NEWLYN, Lucy (Ed.) *Chatter of Choughs: A St. Edmund Hall Anthology of Poems and Essays*, Oxford, 2001.
NEWTON, Lily, *A Handbook of British Seaweeds*, London, 1931.
NISSENSON, Marilyn and JONAS, Susan, *Snake Charm*,

Bibliography and Further Reading

New York, 1995.

NOEL-HUME, Ivor and Audrey, *Tortoises, Terrapins and Turtles*, London, 1958.

PEARSALL, W.H., *Mountains and Moorlands*, revised by Winifred Pennington, London, 1968.

PICKERING, David, *Cassell Dictionary of Witchcraft*, London, 1996.

POLLINGTON, Stephen, *Leechcraft: Early English Charms, Plantlore and Healing*, Norfolk, 2000.

RACKHAM, Oliver, *The History of the Countryside*, London, 1986.

RAMSBOTTOM, John, *Mushrooms and Toadstools: A Study of the Activities of Fungi*, London, 1953.

RÄTSCH, Christian, *Plants of Love: A History of Aphrodisiacs and a Guide to their Identification and Use*, Ten Speed Press, California, undated.

ROBERTS, Michael J., *Collins Field Guide to the Spiders of Britain and Europe*, London, 1995.

ROBIN, P. Ansell, *Animal Lore in English Literature*, London, 1932.

ROPER, Lyndal, 'Witchcraft and the Western Imagination', *Transactions of the Royal Historical Society*, 16 (2006), 117-141.

SANDARS, Edmund, *An Insect Book for the Pocket*, London, 1946.

SAVOURY, Theodore H., *The Spiders and Allied Orders of the British Isles*, London, 1945.

SAX, Boria, *Crow*, London, 2003.

SCHULTES, Richard Evans and HOFMANN, Albert, *Plants of the Gods: their Sacred, Healing and Hallucinogenic Powers*, Vermont, 1992.

SEAFIELD, Lily, *Scottish Ghosts*, New Lanark, 1999.

SHAKESPEARE, William, *Macbeth* (Penguin Popular Classics edition, 1994).

SHARP, William (Ed.) *Lyra Celtica*, Edinburgh, 1932.

SKUTCH, Alexander F., 'Paradoxical Plants', in *Harmony and Conflict in the Living World*, Oklahoma, 2000.
SMITH, Gregor Ian, *Folk Tales of the Highlands*, Edinburgh, 1953.
SMITH, Malcolm, *The British Amphibians and Reptiles*, London, 1969.
SPINAGE, Clive, *Myths and Mysteries of Wayland Smith*, Oxfordshire, 2003.
STEP, Edward, *Wayside and Woodland Ferns*, London, 1945.
STUTESMAN, Drake, *Snake*, London, 2005.
SULLIVAN, Robert, *Rats: A Year with New York's Most Unwanted Inhabitants*, London, 2004.
SUREY-GENT, Sonia and MORRIS, Gordon, *Seaweed: a User's Guide*, London, 1987.
THOMAS, Eric and WHITE, John T., *Hedgerow*, London, 1980.
TUDGE, Colin, *The Secret Life of Trees: How They Live and Why They Matter*, London, 2006.
TURRILL, W.B., *British Plant Life*, London, 1962.
VALIENTE, Doreen, *Witchcraft for Tomorrow*, London, 1978.
VESEY-FITZGERALD, Brian, *British Bats*, London, 1949.
VICKERY Roy, *The Oxford Dictionary of Plant Lore*, Oxford, 1995.
WALKER, John, *A Selection of Curious Articles from the Gentleman's Magazine*, London, 1814.
WATSON, Giles, *Angiosperms: The Secret Lives of Flowering Plants*, in L. Watson and M.J. Dallwitz, 1992 onwards. *The families of flowering plants: descriptions, illustrations, identification, and information retrieval*, Version: 27th April 2006.
WATSON, Giles, *Cryptogams: the Secret Lives of Spore-Bearing Plants*, in Watson, L., and Dallwitz, M.J. 2005 onwards, *The moss families of the British Isles*. Version: 13th April 2007.
WATSON, Giles, *The Secret Lives and Lore of British Land and Freshwater Molluscs*, in Watson, L., and Dallwitz, M.J., 2005 onwards, *The families of British non-marine molluscs (slugs, snails*

Bibliography and Further Reading

and mussels), Version: 13th April 2007.

WATSON, Giles, *The Secret Lives of Insects*, in L. Watson and M. J. Dallwitz (2003 onwards), *British Insects: the Insect Orders*, Version: 9th April 2007.

WATSON, Giles, *The Secret Lives of Spiders*, in Watson, L., and Dallwitz, M.J., 2004 onwards, *The families of spiders represented in the British Isles,.* Version: 13th April 2007.

WESTWOOD, Jennifer and SIMPSON, Jacqueline, *The Lore of the Land: A Guide to England's Legends, from Spring-Heeled Jack to the Witches of Warboys*, London, 2005.

WHEELER, Post (Ed.), *Russian Wonder Tales*, London, 1912.

WHITLOCK, Ralph, *Historic Forests of England*, New Jersey, 1979.

WILBY, Emma, *Cunning Folk and Familiar Spirits: Shamanistic Visionary Traditions in Early Modern Witchcraft and Magic*, Brighton, 2005.

WILLIAMS, Alfred, *Villages of the White Horse*, London, 1913.

WILSON, Bee, *The Hive: The Story of the Honeybee and Us*, London, 2004.

WOOD, Eric S., *Collins Field Guide to Archaeology*, London, 1963.

ZADKIEL and SIBLY, *A Handbook of Dreams and Fortune-Telling*, (undated, C19th), reprinted London, 1994.

Biographical Note

Giles Watson was born in Southampton, but emigrated to Australia with his parents at the age of one, and lived there for the next twenty-five years, before returning to Britain to live successively in Durham, Buckinghamshire and the Isles of Scilly. He has been writing poetry and taking photographs for as long as he can remember, and has more recently experimented with painting and film, in order to indulge his fascination with the relationship between text and image. Giles also writes prose essays on natural history and mediaeval visual culture, is an avid walker and amateur naturalist, and has a keen interest in folklore, art and theatre. As a secondary school teacher, he has taught English, History, Drama, Sociology and Film. He lives in rural Oxfordshire, inspired by his partner Jeannie, and by the ancient and natural history of the region.

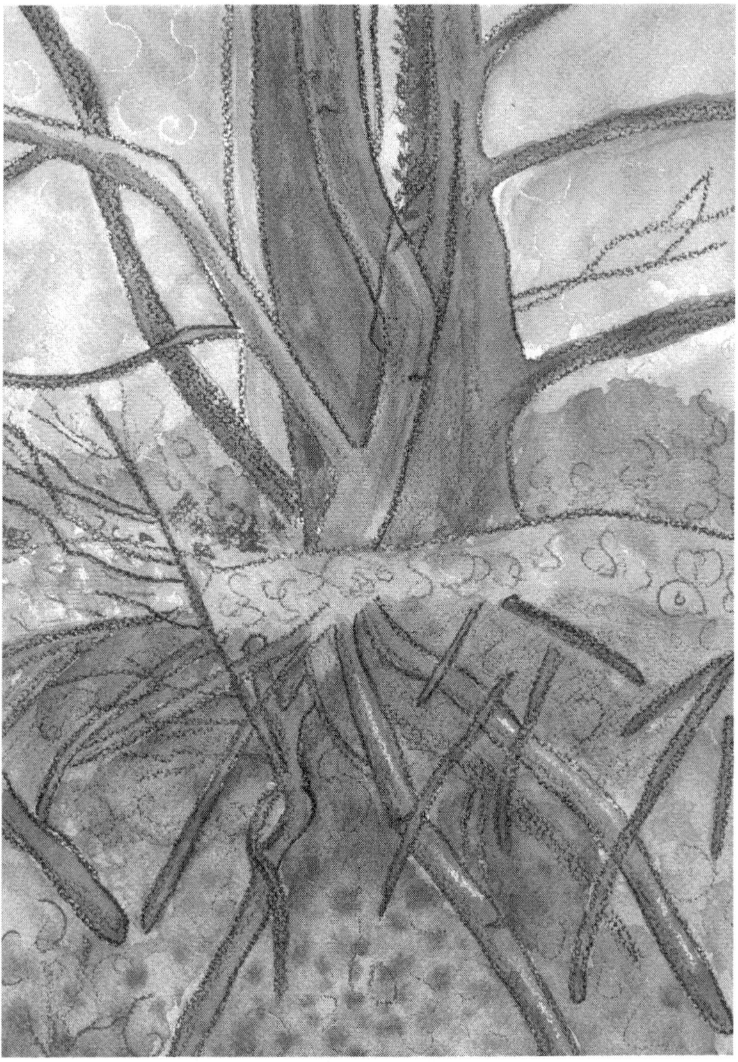

Index

Aboriginal tribesmen, 54
Adder, 68-72, 75-76
Aesop, 97
Agelena labyrinthica, 17
Agraulos, 37
Agrippina, 87
Albertus Magnus, 99
Aldrovandus, 99
Amanita caesarea, 87
Amanita phalloides, 87
Amphibians, 53, 60-61, 63, 156
Antony, St, 89-90
Apamea monoglypha, 26
Apollo, 37, 73
Apples, 109, 125-126
Appolonius of Rhodes, 72
Apuleius, 21, 72, 150
Araneus diadematus, 17
Archaeopteryx, 51
Arion ater, 32
Aristophanes, 47, 59, 150
Arthur, King, 38-39, 42, 71, 154
Asclepius, 73
Ascophyllum nodosum, 136
Ash tree, 109, 129

Index

Athene, 37
Avebury, 147
Axolotls, 61
Baba Yaga, 18, 46, 124-125, 127-131
Bacchanalia, 30
Bacchic and Orphic mysteries, 73
Badbury Rings, 42
Badhbh, 37, 45
Baldr, 116
Barbastelle, 97
Bat, 80, 97-101, 107
Bate, Seldiy, 40, 150
Becket, Thomas, 42
Bedlam, 143
Beech, 35, 129, 140-141
Beetle, 23, 25
Belladonna, 103-104
Bestiaries, 39, 56, 61, 70
Big Raven, 36, 89
Biotoxins, 62
Bishopstone, Wiltshire, 139-141, 144-145
Black Death, 40, 111
Black Shuck, 44
Blackingstone Rock, 41
Blackthorn, 113
Blackthorns, 109
Bladderwort, 120, 123
Blake, William, 74, 78
Blind worm, 69, 80
Blodeuwedd, 51

Bosch, Hieronymus, 57
Botrychium lunaria, 92
Bovet, Richard, 92
Bran, 37
Breton, Louis, 55
Breugel, Pieter, 41
Bride, 51
Brindabella mountains, 54
Bryony, white, 114, 141
Bufo, 62
Buprestid beetles, 26
Burns, Robert, 106
Burton, Tim, 22
Butterfly, 22, 27, 127
Butterwort, 120
Caddis, 26
Cadmus, 73-74
Camlann, 71
Cane toad, 54
Carroll, Lewis, 88
Catweazle, 62
Chalmers, Mary, 141
Charles II, 125
Cheiron, 105
Chelmsford witches, 55
Cherokee, 97-98
Child Ballad, 41
Chough, 42
Christ, 48, 73
Chumbley, Andrew, 58, 151

Index

Churchyard, 49, 95-97, 102, 104-106
Circe, 106
Circe invideosa, 106
Circea, 105
Ciumești, 38
Clare, John, 11, 36, 48, 151
Claudius, 87
Claviceps purpurea, 89
Club mosses, 88, 93
Coatlicue, 72
Coccus polonica, 116
Cochlearium, 30
Cockroach, 27
Conquistadors, 100
Coprinus atramentarius, 88
Coprinus comatus, 87
Cordyceps militaris, 91
Corroboree frog, 54
Corvids, 35-37, 39-42, 151
Cotswolds, 65
Cox, Dame Julian, 55
Crane-fly, 60
Crete, 27
Cricket (bush), 24
Cronus, 37
Crows, 35, 37, 39-40, 42, 144, 151, 154
Cú Chulainn, 38
Culpepper, 32, 92
Cupid and Psyche, 22
Currawong, 35

Dance of Death, 85, 95
Dark Arches, 26
Dawkins, Richard, 11, 13, 61, 152
Deakin, Roger, 126
Death, 41, 83-85, 95-96, 107, 147
Death adder, 67
Devil, 43, 58-59, 74, 79, 81, 90, 92, 102, 113, 140, 143
Dickens, Charles, 36
Dio Cassius, 87
Dioscorides, 70, 105
Diver, Great Northern, 137
Doctrine of Signatures, 70, 93, 117
Dodoens, 90
Doré, Gustave, 54
Drosera, 120
Duncan, Gilly, 79
Dutch Elm Disease, 132
Egypt, 27
Elder, 91, 109, 112-113
Eleusian mysteries, 90
Elks, Thomas, 40
Enchanter's Nightshade, 105
Equisetum hyemale, 93
Ergot, 89-90
Euophrys frontalis, 18
Euripedes, 47
Euripides, 72
Fairies, 31, 59, 106, 113, 134, 151
Falero, Luis Ricardo, 99
Familiar, 13, 40, 55, 64, 79, 81, 101, 157

Index

Familiars, 17, 55-58, 79, 81
Ferns, 88, 91-92, 144, 156
Flower, Joan, 81
Fly (dung), 24
Fox, 35, 107, 130
Foxgloves, 62, 96, 138
Francis, Earl of Bothwell, 79
Frogs, 53-54, 56, 59-62, 66, 151
Gabriel Hounds, 49
Galileo, 103
Galls, 125
Galvin, 76
Garbh Ogh, 121
Geomalacus maculosus, 32
George, St, 73, 140
Gerald of Wales, 51
Gerard, 51, 90, 104, 114-115, 152
Gertrude, St, 83
Gesner, 99
Ginzburg, Carlo, 126, 152
Goldcrests, 49
Gomez-Alonso, Dr. Juan, 100, 152
Gorse, 122
Gowdie, Isobel, 13, 40, 57, 143
Goya, Francisco, 100
Grasshopper, 22
Graves, Robert, 87, 104, 121, 150
Green Knight, 140
Grouse, 122
Gry puvusengree, 31

Grýla, 136
Gwyddbwyll, 38
Gypsy, 30, 99, 154
Hannibal, 71
Hardy, Thomas, 68, 96, 152-153
Hare, 142-143, 145
Harley manuscript, 110
Harrier, hen, 122-123
Hawthorn, 109-110, 112-113, 117
Hazel, 38, 70, 109-110, 114, 117, 128, 141
Healing Aunts of the Isles of Scilly, 134-138
Heath, Robert, 134
Hecate, 72, 120
Hedge, 109-112, 117
Hedgehog/s, 62, 101
Heket, 60
Helix pomatia, 29
Hemlock water dropwort, 133
Henbane, 40, 103-104
Herb Robert, 115
Herodias, 139
Herse, 37
Hindu, 72, 81, 85
Hirneola auricularia-Judae, 91
Holly, 19, 109, 140
Honeysuckle, 114
Hooper's Rule, 109
Horseman's Word, 59
Horsetail, 93
Hudson, W.H, 11, 22, 26-27, 63, 72, 82, 153

Index

Hugin and Munin, 36
Hutton, Mrs, 105
Hyoscyamus, 104
Hypericum, 116-117
Inuit, 37
Ireland, 38, 73, 121
Isle of Wight, 83
Ivy Girl, 114
Iyinx, 48
Jack-by-the-hedge, 29
Jackdaw, 36, 43
Jay, 43
Jefferies, Richard, 11, 153
Jesus, 37
Jonson, Ben, 60, 98
Karni Mater, 82
Kelp, 134-136, 138
Koryac, 36, 89
Koryak, 89
Labourd witches, 56-57
Lancre, Pierre de, 57
Lehmannia marginata, 32
Leucobryum, 35
Linnaeus, Carl, 53
Linyphia, 18
Lizards, 75-76, 151
Lorenz, Konrad, 36
Lucanus cervus, 25
Lychgate, 95-96, 107
Lycopodium, 93

Mabey, Richard, 11, 116, 151, 154
Mabinogion, 38-39, 51, 152
Macbeth, 40, 68, 78-80, 120-123
Magpie, 13, 43-44
Mandela, Nelson, 42
Maple, 109
Marasmius oreades, 91
Marie de France, 128, 154
Meadow cranesbill, 115
Medea, 72
Medusa, 72-73
Melampus, 105
Melangell, St, 143
Meloe violaceus, 23
Menocchio, 126
Metamorphoses, 26, 73, 98
Midgard Serpent, 73
Milton, John, 57
Minyas, 98
Misumena vatia, 18
Mithras, 37
Morrigu, 37-38
Moth, 21-22, 25-26, 49, 106
Mother Carey, 50-51
Mother Goose, 139, 145
Mouse, long-tailed field, 102
Moytura, 38
Mushrooms, 62, 87, 89-91
Mustelids, 128
Myrtle, bog, 121

Index

Necrophorus, 25
Neoteny, 61
Newts, 53, 61, 63
Nightjars, 48-49
Normans, 110
Oak Apple Day, 125-126
Odin, 36
Oil beetle, 23
Olaus Magnus, 49, 55
Orchid, 25, 127, 129-130
Orkneys, 136
Ormerod, Miss, 63
Orpheus, 73
Osmunda regalis, 93
Ovid, 37, 51, 73, 98
Ovum anguinis, 75
Owl, 51, 80, 107, 117
Owls, 46, 48-49, 140
Oxychilus allarius, 29
Pandrosos, 37
Paracelsus, 117
Pardosa amentata, 19
Patrick, St, 73
Pengersick Castle, 42
Pennant, Thomas, 63-64
Petrel, 50
Phallus impudicus, 90
Physa fontinalis, 32
Pied Piper of Hamelin, 83
Pinguicula, 120

Pipistrelle, 97
Pisaura mirabilis, 19
Pliny, 29, 61, 70-71, 99
Pobblebonk, 53
Poe, Edgar Allan, 41, 84
Polyporus squamosus, 91
Pompeii, 73
Pond skater, 25
Prentice, Joan, 13, 55
Privet, 109
Puritan, 92, 126
Purple Emperor butterfly, 127
Pythons, 74
Quetzalcoatl, 22
Rabies, 100-101
Ragwort, 106
Ramsons, 29
Rat, brown and black, 78, 80-81
Raven, 36-39, 41, 80, 89, 148-149
Reynard the Fox, 130
Rhodymenia palmata, 135
Ridgeway, 139-142, 144, 147
Robin Goodfellow, 115
Romans, 29, 41, 48, 71, 75, 143
Rook, 40, 42
Rosamond, Fair, 58
Rowan, 122
Russia, 98
Russley Downs, 141, 142
Sabbat, 11-12, 17, 22, 40, 54, 57, 96, 104, 107, 145

Index

Sabbat herbs, 104
Salem witch trials, 90
Samhain, 49, 96, 106, 139
Sampson, Agnes, 79, 85
Samson, Isles of Scilly, 136-138
Satan, 57, 98
Scathophaga stercoraria, 24
Scot, Reginald, 116
Scotch pine, 131
Scytodes thoracica, 18
Seal, grey, 133
Seaweed, 135-136
Seven Whistlers, 51
Sexton beetle, 25, 146
Shakespeare, 39, 41, 63, 78-80, 91, 155
Shrews, 101
Sibly, 44, 106, 157
Sicily, 98
Skeleton, 53, 95, 117, 146-147, 149
Sloane, Sir Hans, 114
Sloe, 141
Slow worm, 69
Snail (garlic), 29
Snail (Roman), 29
Snake, 29, 48, 55, 67-69, 71-76, 80
Snake (grass), 69, 75-76
Snakes, 12, 53, 66-68, 71-76, 146
Solanaceae, 103
Sphagnum, 53, 93, 122
Spider, 12, 17-19

Spider (crab), 18
Spider (garden), 17
Spider (jumping), 18
Spider (labyrinth), 17
Spider (money), 18
Spider (spitting), 18
Spider (wolf), 19
Spindle, 12, 109, 113, 122, 128, 141
Stag 25, 121
Stag beetle, 25
St. John's Wort, 115-117
St. Mary's, Isles of Scilly, 133
Stoat, 35, 128
Suetonius, 87
Sumatra, 26
Sundew, 120-121
Tacitus, 87
Taipan, 67
Tarot, 83, 95
Testacella spp, 32
Tettigonia viridissima, 24
Theridion, 18
Toad, 13, 54-64, 79, 141, 151-152
Toad bone amulet, 58-59
Toadmen, 58, 63
Topsell, Edward, 101
Tormentil, 121
Toshers, 82
Tresco, 136
Trotman, John, 42

Trows, 136
Tutankhamun, 27
Twayblades, 125, 140
Twybill, 111
Uffington White Horse, 140-142, 151
Utricularia, 120
Vahinin, 89
Valiente, Doreen, 142, 156
Vampire, 18, 29, 100
Varro, 29
Venus Nights, 114
Verethragna, 37
Ward, Frederick William Orde, 84
Wasp, 22, 125
Wassilissa the Beautiful, 124, 132
Waterhouse, William, 106
Waterton, Charles, 80
Weir, Major Thomas, 113
Weyland the Smith, 140
Weyland's Smithy, 141
Whelk, 71, 75
White, Gilbert, 11
Wild Hunt, 49, 139
William of Malmesbury, 36
Witches, 13, 17-18, 22, 30, 32, 37, 40, 43, 51, 54-57, 62-64, 68, 77-82, 85, 88, 92, 99, 101, 103, 106, 112-113, 117, 120, 122-123, 125, 139, 142-143, 147
Wolves, 99-100
Woodcock, 49-50, 137
Woodpeckers, 47-48

Wormwood, 105
Wryneck, 48
Yarrow, 106
Yew, 96-97, 102, 131
Zadkiel, 44, 96-97, 157
Zeus, 47-48
Zombie, 54